I Like Me Anyway

Embracing Imperfection, Connection & Christ

BROOKE ROMNEY

www.BrookeRomney.com

Printed in the United States of America

First Edition
10 9 8 7 6 5 4 3 2 1

Library of Congress data has been applied for.

ISBN 978-1-7358544-0-3 (Paperback)
ISBN 978-1-7358544-1-0 (eBook)
ISBN 978-1-7358544-2-7 (Audiobook)

"If a book could be your best friend, this is it. Wherever you are on your perfectly imperfect journey, Brooke Romney lovingly designed this book to make a difference in your daily life. Relatable real-life stories on every page will remind you of your worth, your power, and the overflowing grace you can access right now. Simple exercises at the end of each chapter give practical ideas for increasing your personal peace. If you have ever felt overwhelmed, underprepared, or out of your league in life, I can't recommend this book enough."

–**Emily Orton**, *Author of Seven at Sea*

This book is dedicated to every woman who has ever wondered if she was enough...

_____

Prologue

There is something about obscure women in the scriptures. I want to dig in, get to know them, walk beside them, see if we could have been friends. Their brief appearances always leave me wishing for more of their stories.

In Matthew, there is a miracle performed by Jesus for a woman with an issue of blood. She occupies only a few Biblical verses, but she dominated my thoughts for days. Her "issue of blood" most likely meant her menstrual bleeding was unpredictable or unstoppable, rendering her stuck in a life she never planned for, hoped for, or wanted—because of something completely out of her control.

By tradition and the Mosaic law, she was considered unclean and would have been banished from everyday society. Desperate for help, she spent her money visiting doctors and pleading for a cure, but the scriptures tell us none was found. My heart broke for her. I wanted so badly to know her name. I am certain people she didn't know, and many of those she did—her own people—looked down on her with a loss of respect and a hearty helping of pity. How many of her dreams had been put on hold? Those 12 years of trouble and heartache must have felt like an eternity.

But then, in the 9th chapter of Matthew, we read:

> **20** And, behold, a woman, which was diseased with an issue of blood twelve years, came behind *him,* and touched the hem of his garment:
> **21** For she said within herself, If I may but touch his garment, I shall be whole.
> **22** But Jesus turned him about, and when he saw her, he said, Daughter, be of good comfort; thy faith hath made thee whole. And the woman was made whole from that hour.

As I read those verses, two words stopped me in my tracks: "within herself." *For she said, WITHIN HERSELF, if I may but touch his garment, I shall be whole.* The script in her mind was powerful truth. This nameless woman, who had every excuse to feel worthless and undeserving, knew within herself that she was worthy of the Savior.

Society had taught her to feel low; the law had declared her unclean. She had so many reasons to shrink into the shadows. She knew she would be ridiculed for seeking and touching someone like Jesus, but she paid no attention to the naysayers. She created her own holy mantra, one that kept her moving forward even when the world built walls around her.

There was a fire inside of her, a light that would not be extinguished. She bravely walked down the congested streets, intently fought her way through the crushing crowd, and humbly crawled those last few, lonely feet, so she could have her moment with Jesus.

How did she know that she was deserving of her Savior's healing and love? What had she been taught as a child that shaped her confidence? What had she read and learned that solidified her worth?

She must have been a woman who embraced imperfection and the unexpected, who consistently connected herself to what was most important, and who had the courage to reach for Jesus and invite Him into *her* story. She was a woman who experienced the impossible, because deep down she knew something important, something true, WITHIN HERSELF.

We rise when we focus on what we can give.

CHAPTER 1

How Do You Do It All?

I had my first baby just outside Washington, D.C., 3,000 miles away from family and friends. This was in the early 2000s, long before the advent of blogs and social media, which was a good thing because motherhood, something I thought would be so care-free and natural, was anything but easy-breezy for me. There were few picture-perfect moments and certainly nothing graceful or #goals about it.

I remember trying to swaddle my baby in the hospital after I changed his diaper for the first time. The nurses made it look simple, but when it was my turn, the results were so embarrassing, I blamed the sadly wadded up blanket bundle on my husband. I couldn't nurse without removing all of my clothing and using 6 different pillows, and I didn't know what to do with that crazy umbilical cord or have any techniques for safely giving a baby boy a bath. When I dropped my mom off at the airport 10 days later, I had to pull over because I couldn't see the road through my tears.

I remember calling my husband, Mike, frantically sobbing into my flip phone while the baby screamed from the back. He thought there had been a horrible accident, but instead I said, "I just dropped my mom off at the airport, and I have no idea how to do any of this!"

He was relieved that the crisis was rather ordinary, and talked me down from that metaphorical ledge. I made it home and began my motherhood experiment all by myself.

It's hard to even imagine in our super connected world, but I was pretty much on my own. Mike was commuting into the city and gone for 12–15 hours at a time, and I had few friends and no family. I remember looking at my chubby little boy and thinking, "So, what are we going to do together all day?" The Internet was rather new, and Google hadn't come on the scene yet, so being distracted by a screen wasn't an option. This made motherhood a little lonely and a lot difficult, but having the chance to figure it out on my own was a surprising blessing. With hours trapped in our basement condo, I began to grow and discover myself.

I watched episode after episode of *Trading Spaces* and ended up faux painting the heck out of our apartment. I bought some Bohemian pillows from Pier One, added a red wall to our kitchen, and crackle-painted an old bookcase. As I looked around, I felt incredibly satisfied. I was certain I was destined to be a design star.

I watched a lot of Food Network and learned a few fancy tricks to make everything taste "semi-home-made." Our dinners had never been better, and I took great pride in making frozen chicken topped with canned spaghetti sauce and melted mozzarella cheese. My own gourmet chicken parmesan. Delicious.

I read lots of parenting books and followed them as best I could. My baby still cried almost constantly and was only happy in my arms or outside. But I felt like a motherhood rockstar rotating tummy time, board books, and constant feedings, just like the experts prescribed.

I made some friends, set up a few play dates, and enjoyed walks and conversation with women who were a few steps ahead of me. They took me in as the "young new mom," and I felt cared for and loved as they taught me their tips and tricks for surviving that first year.

I even figured out how to keep our floors vacuumed and get the clothes from the washer to the dryer before they smelled like mildew—no easy feat on the humid East Coast. My level of homemaking was at an all-time high. I was exceedingly proud and happy in my new role as a stay-at-home mom . . . pleased with all I had learned and the progress I had made in such a short amount of time.

When my oldest was 15 months, we decided to move from Virginia to Arizona, into a Stepford-like neighborhood full of hundreds of young families in similar houses with small yards and shared common areas. Almost everyone we met was pretty much just like us. Young, new homeowners, with a child or two or three.

They were good and kind, and they welcomed us with open arms and invitations to dinner, playgroups, and dessert in their homes. As we traveled from house to house, my circle grew, but my worth subtly and slowly decreased.

Their houses were decorated beautifully, not just hodgepodged together like mine. They served home-made bread and authentic Mexican food. They canned fruit, made extravagant birthday cakes, and had photography businesses on the side. Their houses were clean enough for me to walk upstairs without warning, and doors were opened to made beds and organized toys. They were patient and calm parents to multiple children and had chore charts and family home evening kits. They showed us where they put their three months of food storage and all their camping supplies.

After each visit, I would return home and wonder how in the world they did it all. My walls were bare, I was afraid of yeast, and I would rather cut off an arm than let someone walk upstairs without warning. I thought food storage and canning were things only elderly people did, and I had never even heard of "family home evening packets."

In a matter of one month, I went from thinking I was a motherhood guru to wondering how I would ever keep up. I hadn't lost my talents or my knowledge, but I had started comparing myself to others, and not even to just one person, but to a conglomeration of everyone's best talents and attributes. I felt completely worthless.

And so I sank. I pouted. I stuck to myself, not wanting anyone to see how devoid I was of the things that made other women so special. I was in a serious rut, and felt lonely all over again, this time because of my own choice to distance myself from those who seemed so much better than I was at everything.

Then one day, right in the middle of a "poor me" moment, the Spirit said, loudly, "Knock it off." He reminded me that **maybe I wasn't good at everything, but I had gifts to share.** Maybe I couldn't quilt, but I could gather women. Maybe my drawers weren't organized, but I was outgoing and friendly. Maybe I wasn't going to win a baking contest, but I could chat. And so, instead of moping, I began using my talents.

I organized playgroups and park days. I led a neighborhood Exercise class I wasn't qualified to lead, and planned pool time and outings to local children's spots. I involved anyone and everyone and encouraged women to get out and be together. I helped create unity and cohesion in a place that really needed it. And you know what? Getting out there and using my gifts changed the way I felt about everything.

Maybe you too are stuck in a comparison rut that is beating you down. Perhaps you are sure that other mothers or grandmothers or employees have it all together while you are barely staying afloat. Can I lovingly ask you to change that narrative? We all have talents *and* we all struggle, but **we rise when we focus on what we *can* give.**

So, what are you good at? What do you enjoy doing? What do you want to learn more about? How can you grow and share the talents you currently have? Pray for guidance and listen for answers.

This exact process helped me realize that I did have worth. **Even if my contribution looked a little different, a little less organized, and a little**

more messy than everyone else's, it was still important. *I* was still important. And, when I recognized my worth, it changed my heart.

Instead of seeing women as competitors or enemies, I saw them as friends and allies. I realized that God had given me the priceless gift of planting me in a fishbowl of creative excellence, so I could take the opportunity to improve myself.

The six years I was in Arizona turned into the most wonderful learning lab. I learned to make cinnamon rolls and can food and decorate and organize and teach and love in ways I had never thought myself capable of. No one would ever accuse me of being the BEST or the MOST TALENTED at any of it, but I was a better version of myself, and that felt good.

I can't imagine what my life would be like now, had I chosen to pout and feel sorry for myself during that time. What precious opportunities, what gratifying friendships I would have missed out on!

Our spirits crave learning, creation, and growth because we are daughters of an Almighty Learner and Creator. When we allow ourselves to do those same things, we are more in touch with our true, eternal selves. **We don't gain more worth by being more talented**, but when we improve ourselves and become closer to our Heavenly Parents in that process of growth and struggle, our hearts change and allow us to appreciate our own worth and the worth of others like never before.

————

Exercise #1

Make a list of your talents and gifts. Decide on one you would like to work on this week. Notice how it brings you joy.

_____

_____

_____

_____

_____

_____

Exercise #2

Is there someone you feel jealous or envious of? What could you learn from her? Sometime this month, invite her to share a meal with you or ask her to teach you something new.

_____

_____

_____

_____

_____

_____

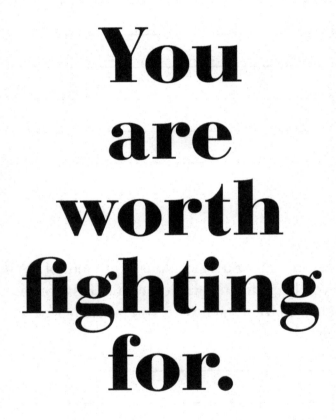

CHAPTER 2

Does God Care?

The only constant in my life has been unpredictability. Just when I think I have things figured out, just when I am sure of who I am, I discover a new weakness.

I remember as a teen, hearing about people who had abandoned their faith. I always wondered, "How?! How could they ever . . . ?" Growing up, doing the right thing felt good, so it was easy to stay on the path. In addition to that, Jesus Christ was central to the joy in my life and a guiding and uniting pillar in my family. I could not imagine another way. Until I could.

A few years ago, a handful of individuals I greatly respect began to question my Church and many of its policies. I had always admired the way they thought through important issues, and though there was no pressure from them to undo my faith, I started to waver. Because I have a questioning, curious, and logical mind, I wanted to understand where they were coming from. I found their ideas fresh, interesting, and worth investigating. So, I spent hours each day immersed in their dialogues, following their logic and links, and giving credence to their opinions, *all the while forgetting about my own personal study* and the many spiritual witnesses I had personally received throughout my life. Instead, I began to quietly focus on what bothered me about the gospel.

Well, what we seek, we find. And as the Cherokee legend goes, **the wolf you feed is the one that wins**, **and my doubts and fears had a steady diet while my faith was starving.** I went to church out of habit, but almost everything that was said bothered me. My temple sessions were Spiritless, and I constantly felt like I was just going through the motions, at one point, even pretending. My prayers began to be testy and infrequent, as if I were challenging God to figure it all out for me.

I remember thinking that if Heavenly Father really loved me and cared about me, and if He wanted me to have a testimony, He would give it to me. I wanted Him to directly answer all my questions, perhaps even send an angel, so I could close this difficult, doubting chapter. I wondered why He wanted everyone else to happily feel part of His gospel family, but not me. Didn't I matter to Him anymore? Didn't He want ME?

During this time, it was interesting what I continued to hold on to. I had taken a challenge to read the entire Book of Mormon, and while I wasn't reading with any real intent or enthusiasm, I kept plugging along.

Church attendance was also habitual, something I had always done. So I showed up each Sunday with a dress and a smile on the outside, even though inside I was restless and cynical.

I continued to fulfill my Primary calling, mostly out of duty, but something changed for me when I entered that little room each week. I taught the eight-year-olds, and that year we were studying the New Testament. Try as I might to remain hard-hearted, the stories about Jesus, His love, and the simplicity of His message touched me as I shared them with the eager boys and girls on plastic chairs. They believed.

I remember wishing I could go back to a time when everything seemed so simple, when the only important doctrine was, "I am a child of God." I heard a faint whisper: "Why can't you?"

There were other small, sacred moments over the next few months that started to thaw my cold heart, allowing the Spirit in a little at a time. As this softening started to happen, it all began to make sense.

I realized that God DID want me. He had been quietly, consistently fighting for me all along.

He never took away my agency or forced me to believe, but He did fight for me—through that Book of Mormon challenge, through a patient and loving husband who didn't mind my barrage of unfriendly questions, through children who craved gospel truth, through a Primary calling that brought me back to the foundations of the gospel, and through talks and lessons that reached me, even when I pretended to be too intelligent to care.

When I understood that I mattered to Him, my heart began to change, to soften, and to heal. I was again able to see joy in the restored gospel and began to make peace with some of my questions. I started to focus on what I knew and loved about His church and remembered the witnesses that had been a part of my own faith story. I stopped kicking against the pricks and was content to "be still" for a while and trust in God and His timing.

Maybe you have been where I was, or maybe you are there right now. Maybe you are burdened with depression or anxiety that seems to block your ability to feel the Spirit and God's love, with sin that seems too heavy and hard to shake, with doubts that consume your heart and mind, or with a life experience that takes your breath and hope away. But please, hold on.

These experiences can make the Spirit feel dull or far away, which allows us to conclude that maybe we aren't worthy enough, righteous enough, happy enough, or faithful enough for God to want us. I want you to know He is still fighting for you, just like He fought for me.

Think of the times when you heard a talk just in the nick of time, when a neighbor eased your burdens, when a feeling of love flooded over you when you felt you were undeserving, when someone gave you a second chance and a flicker of hope, when an unknowing friend called while you were feeling alone, or when Jesus Christ started to work in your life. My friends, these moments are not coincidences. That is your Heavenly Father trying to help you understand how much you mean to Him—that **YOU are worth fighting for**.

So**, plug along in those holy habits**, even when you don't feel like it. Those small, daily actions that I continued to choose, saved me. I will be forever grateful that I never stopped "going through the motions."

When I felt a little more confident in my spirituality, those little efforts led to bigger actions. I started to fill my life with uplifting articles and podcasts. I made time for the scriptures and had conversations on faith. I realized that reaping what we sow is an eternal truth. **Cultivating goodness and a testimony takes work, time, and sacrifice, and the outcome, though slow, is life changing.**

But if you still feel like God doesn't really care about you or your place in His gospel, please reach out. Open up. Confide in a friend or a church leader. Find a professional. Everyone has struggles and lows, but they can unite us in hope and faith if we let them. **I am certain that we were never meant to go through our hardest times or faith crises alone**.

Knowing you matter to God makes everything bearable. That knowledge is worth figuring out, worth working for. Your Savior is fighting for you. He knows about your addiction, your husband who no longer believes, your child who is making poor choices, the financial trouble you are in—and **He wants you anyway**. He will take you as you are, and start you on a path to something better. Just reach for Him, and He will take care of the rest.

Exercise #1

Write about a time when you know your Heavenly Father fought for you. How does remembering this make you feel?

_____

_____

_____

_____

_____

Exercise #2

What types of holy habits do you need to add to your daily life? Choose something you will do this week that will bolster your personal faith journey.

_____

_____

_____

_____

_____

True worth comes from believing, with certainty, that you are known and loved by God.

CHAPTER 3

Hey, Give Me Back My Worth!

It seems to be human nature to attach our worth to the people around us. For some reason, as parents, it is particularly easy to allow our children's actions to determine how we feel about ourselves.

If we raise 4.0 students, our worth shoots up. If we get a call from the principal, our worth goes down. Someone lands the lead in the school musical, we are on top of the world. If they get cut from the team, we want to hide. Raising kids who are kind and helpful makes us feel so satisfied with ourselves, but if others don't seem to like them, we hang our heads and wonder what went wrong.

If I am honest, even writing this chapter feels a bit hypocritical. It's just so dang fun when our kids succeed, and it hurts so badly when they fail. It seems almost impossible to not take it all personally. I have spent a good portion of motherhood wrestling with my worth because my kids don't always follow the path I prescribe for them. I know better cerebrally, but every disappointment is still painfully hard.

When my youngest was in first grade, his teacher pulled me aside to let me know that multiple parents had complained about him being mean at recess. Now, this little guy is the youngest of four boys, and I am not a stranger to the principal's office or emails from teachers, but the hard stuff never started as early as first grade. To make matters worse, he was really easy at home, so I was blindsided by the news. I was so shocked, I didn't even know what to do or what to say, so I apologized profusely and said we would take care of things.

When I arrived home, I did what I assume most parents do with bad news about their child. First, I rationalized. "Parents are so sensitive these days. The people complaining are probably parents of first children or they must have all girls." I did my best to salvage my worth by diminishing the worth of others, but, surprise! That only made me feel worse. So, I tried feeling sorry for myself instead. I had already had a rough week with another child with a big personality, and so I asked Heavenly Father, "Why me? How come my friends get all the easy kids? Why don't their kids ever make things hard? It's not fair."

But playing comparison and "it's not fair" games with God is a losing battle. And so, in frustration,

I gave up and just wallowed in it. I beat myself up all night, questioning every choice I had made over the last seven years as his parent. I was sure I was a failure as a mother for all kinds of reasons, and I felt so sorry for myself and my kids who had to deal with all my shortcomings.

As I listened to our church's general conference the next morning, I was really hoping for a boost, maybe an "it's fine if your kids are mean" sermon straight from the pulpit, but instead I felt lower and lower as I heard stories of successful parents who seemed to do it all right. I said to myself, "Even when you are trying your very hardest, you are still failing. Maybe you're just no good at this parenting thing."

When my husband walked in from a business trip halfway through the session and found me angry cleaning, he knew something was up. As I unloaded my inadequacies onto his shoulders, the Spirit spoke to my mind and heart. It reminded me of where all my previous thoughts were coming from, and then it clearly taught me truth.

The Spirit helped me understand that I *was* trying to teach my boys goodness and kindness, but that they were also born with their own personalities, strengths, and weaknesses. I heard the Spirit clearly say to me, "Pierce doesn't struggle with reading or math or playing sports, but he does struggle with

21

being kind. So, you are going to have to work at it and teach it and check up on it just like you would if he couldn't read. Kindness doesn't come easily to him, but he can learn to be kind."

I fought with the Spirit just a bit . . . "Isn't being an example good enough? No one else has to specifically teach kindness, do they?" But then I humbled myself. I would teach it, just like I would teach any other skill. It might take a while or a lifetime, and he might not ever be perfect at it, but I would teach him because I love him.

I felt inspired to change some things in our home and asked the older boys to buy in. We talked about how their tone, sarcasm, and words were being absorbed by a little brother, and how 16-year-old trash talk didn't translate well on a first-grade playground. They were all willing to help and try to improve themselves in the process.

As I read my scriptures that week, I ran across 1 Nephi chapter 3, verse 8. This is after Lehi had asked his boys to go back to Jerusalem to get the plates, and Laman and Lemuel didn't want to go. Then, we see Nephi stepping up, choosing to go and do the things the Lord asked of him. Lehi's reaction to Nephi's obedience was:

"When my father had heard these words he was exceedingly glad, for he knew that I had been blessed of the Lord."

This scriptural insight was another affirmation of the Spirit during a tough time. Lehi didn't sit and beat himself up because two of his sons were stubborn and unwilling to follow the Lord's commandments, but he also didn't pat himself on the back about what a great job he had done with Nephi. No, he thanked the Lord for the good and continued to teach and love them all the best way he knew how. Lehi personally chose to live a life of gratitude and one that followed the direction of the Lord, and because of that, he had peace and confidence in his parenting.

It made me think that maybe I could do the same. Maybe I could be more diligent about thanking the Lord for the goodness in my children. And then, like Lehi, continue to teach and love with confidence even when it seemed like no progress was being made. It had to be worth a try.

I remember, as a young mom, complimenting a friend on what an amazing job she was doing with her teenage son. She wisely replied, **"If I take credit for all the good, then I also have to take credit for all the bad. So each day I just try to show up for them, love them, and teach them the best way I know how. The rest is up to them."**

Having this confidence, this trust in the process, requires us to distance ourselves from the eyes of the world and realize that, as parenting expert Ralphie Jacobs says, **"Parenting is not a social matter." We must remember that parenting is a personal, spiritual, and emotional matter.**[1]

It is natural to want to look like a good parent, but oftentimes the best parents don't always look good to the outside world. They make the hard choices, go against the grain, are humiliated and humbled by embarrassing moments, and make a million mistakes, but they practice spirit driven parenting, do their best, and press on.

Through a lot of internal searching, fasting, and prayer, I have come to the conclusion that we can all consider ourselves successful parents even when the outcome is pretty ugly at the moment. If you are loving, trying, forgiving, failing, learning, and trying again, stop beating yourself up. **Each of your children has a unique purpose in God's grand plan, and surprisingly enough, we can't always see the outcome while battling in the trenches.**

---

1 *Dalquist, Jessica. "Episode 176: Parenting on Purpose with Ralphie Jacobs." Extraordinary Moms. [Podcast Audio], October 17, 2007. https://extraordinarymomspodcast.com/ralphie/.*

It's good to remind ourselves that children are supposed to make mistakes and test boundaries and make their parents lose sleep at night. Agency was the ultimate principle of our Savior's plan, so we must honor it in our own lives and in our own families. If we wallowed, pouted, took it personally, and let it subtract from our worth every time our child didn't obey or excel, parenting would be a rather miserable endeavor.

So, instead, try to enjoy your children. Don't throw in the towel at 6, 16, 26, or 56. **There is a lot of life to live and an incredible amount of time for them to grow into their own greatness.** Try seeing them (and yourself) through God's eyes. It changes everything.

Even when you are working especially hard to stay grounded, parenting can be so confusing. You see one set of parents that breaks all the "good parenting" rules and neglects spiritual consistency, yet their kids turn out strong and faithful. Another set of parents seems to do everything right; they are full of kindness, dedication and spirituality, yet they struggle with child after child. I had such a hard time understanding why this happens, until I remembered that **we are all here as brothers and sisters**, not as parents and children. And we have a Heavenly Father that desperately wants each of us to return to Him.

Because of this, He wisely gives *all* of us the best chance at having the right experiences and people in our lives, so we can make it back. Maybe some parents need spiritually-strong children with an excess of faith to support them on their path of righteousness, while others need challenging children who allow them to learn humility and reliance on the Lord. Perhaps one child is gifted with grit and optimism and is capable of charting her own course, while another needs a parent who can patiently love him through unimaginable, personal lows.

There is purpose to this plan, and I've learned to rely on a God who is good and gives us each exactly what we need to become the people He knows we can be. **We can choose to feel defeated because of parenting struggles or choose to see unimaginable miracles in less-than-ideal circumstances. I choose to trust that God knows me personally and is present in the details of our lives.**

This idea was taught so beautifully to my friend Sharon (name has been changed). It was a crucial yet painful moment that reminded her of Heavenly Father's unconditional love and willingness to teach us through our children.

Sharon's son left on a mission along with the slew of

other excited 18-year-olds graduating high school. Three months later, he was back home because of past transgressions that hadn't been resolved. His parents were devastated and embarrassed. Their neighbors avoided their eyes and gossiped, and one even reprimanded them, telling them what they could have done and should have known. Sharon spent the first week he was home upset and emotional, certain no one would ever see their family the same again. That weekend, her son came to her and said he was going to go watch his old high school play their Friday night football game, and wondered if his parents wanted to come.

She was shocked and dismayed. She told him he couldn't go . . . they couldn't go. She was mortified at the thought of the entire community seeing him back home. Her son looked his mother in the eyes and said, "I am working things out with the Lord. This is between the two of us. If anyone else has a problem with me, they can work it out with Him, too."

That night, they all walked into the football game with their heads held high. Sharon's son was her hero that day as he taught her what worth truly means. **Real worth cannot come from the approval of others, from accolades or awards; true worth comes from knowing, with certainty, that you are known and loved by God.**

Exercise #1

How have you allowed the actions of others to take away or determine your worth? Do some thought work as you separate your worth and life from the life choices and agency of others.

_____

_____

_____

_____

_____

Exercise #2

Think of a time when despite your best efforts, you didn't attain your desired outcome. Make a list of what you were especially proud of through that situation.

_____

_____

_____

_____

_____

Being less than perfect is perfectly okay.

CHAPTER 4

Over-Processed, Over-Done, & Glammed Out

There are times when I feel the pull of the world so strongly, when the unimportant things seem to consume my thoughts and my time so easily, it feels like the only option. Our current landscape is saturated with materialism and superficiality, and it's almost impossible not to be swept up in the crowd of glamour, beauty, and fun.

When I personally need to be tethered to what truly matters, I look to others who have weathered this challenge by holding on with grace. My mom has always been a steady and immovable example when it comes to resisting the things of the world. She has a little curve on the tip of her nose that she affectionately calls "The Cullimore Hook." She has wrinkles on her face, a flat chest, a great smile, and incredible legs.

In today's world, full of over-processed, overdone,

and glammed-out women, I will be forever grateful that I was raised by a mother who has always been too busy with important things to scrutinize every inch of her body, to obsess about fine lines, to turn herself into something she isn't.

Growing up, we shopped together at inexpensive stores, where she taught me how to dress for my shape, look for items that were stylish but on sale, and buy only outfits I was sure I would wear. Brands didn't matter, and clothes were fun but never used as a status symbol. Our outings were enjoyable but not excessive.

I remember wondering why she didn't wear more makeup, get her nails done, or wear heels all the time. I was aching to be able to do all those things and couldn't imagine why she would pass up an opportunity to be more chic, but all those things just weren't her.

Beauty was never the focus. It was assumed that we would look put together and situationally appropriate, but there was no expectation to be beautiful. My mom understood that **beauty is subjective and fleeting, and attaching ourselves to something so capricious will only end in disappointment.**

Today, as a grandma, she is just as real. She smiles

for pictures when she is makeup free and is confident and comfortable with who she is: a woman who has never defined herself by what she looks like, but always by what she gives.

I had no idea what an impact her little choices and quiet example to be her true best self would have on me as I became an adult. When budgets were tight, our funds weren't siphoned toward spa appointments or department-store makeup. In the early years of marriage, I didn't feel the pressure to spend money that we didn't have in order to keep up a certain appearance. And as my face and body have changed with age, I see it as a natural occurrence instead of something to fight against.

I have varicose veins that scare children, love handles I can't help but pinch, stretch marks like cat scratches, and plenty of wrinkles already, but it's all just fine. My mom taught me that **being less than perfect is perfectly okay.** That my body is a gift and worth taking care of, but moderation is necessary. She showed me that the fountain of youth is not found in a bottle or needle, but in a childlike heart and genuine smile.

Because of her, I know that real beauty is having a life purpose that allows you to brush aside the unimportant, and that being anxiously engaged in fulfilling causes, keeps me from searching for happiness in places it doesn't exist. She taught me that **a new outfit can be a great pick-me-up, but nothing takes you higher than knowing you are right with God**.

It's hard to ever measure up to your mom. In fact, there may come a day when I laser those pesky varicose veins, add some eyelashes, or get my nails done. But because of her, I know that smooth legs, sultry eyes, and French tips have nothing to do with who I really am. **What defines me is how I love, who I serve, and what I create with this precious body and little time I am given.**

Her example has been invaluable. But even with it, I am often still weak, swayed by magazine covers, Instagram posts, before-and-after photos, and every exciting fad that comes along. When I lose my focus and start to get caught up in worldly thinking that diminishes my worth, I like to remember what the Lord said to an exceptionally valiant Emma Smith in Doctrine and Covenants 25:3, 10:

> "Thou art an elect lady whom I have called. . . . I say unto thee that thou shalt lay aside the things of this world, and seek for the things of a better."

About six years ago, I heard that same message, though it sounded a bit more modern in my ears. I had been asked to be on a local TV show to discuss an article I had written.

I was over the moon at my very first invitation to be on TV! I spent the majority of the week worrying about what I was going to wear, getting my hair colored, shopping, and borrowing jewelry. As I was trying on outfits, a voice came into my mind: "Brooke, they aren't bringing you on because of the way you look. They want you to share your message. Focus on what's important."

That impression has revisited me over and over again. **It is so easy to focus on the trivial, the things that don't really matter, at the expense of what really does**. If you struggle with similar thoughts, let me remind you that **you were not put on this earth just to look pretty or to slink in the shadows of insecurity**. You were put here because you have something divine to contribute to this world. You have talents, gifts, and ways of reaching people that no one else has. So please, don't, as President Monson said, "immerse [yourself] in the thick of thin things."[2]
Don't stay quiet because the numbers on the scale aren't where they used to be. Don't keep

---

2 *Thomas S. Monson, "What Have I Done for Someone Today?" Ensign, November 2009:* https://www.churchofjesuschrist.org/study/general-conference/2009/10/what-have-i-done-for-someone-to-day?lang=eng

to yourself because your home is too small or too messy. Don't hide your talents because you don't have the right outfit to share them in. Don't hold back your smile because you think your face is too wrinkled to spark joy.

Remember, your Heavenly Father put you here to share your message, your gifts, your light. If you need courage or a reminder of who you are and whose you are, ask Him what you have to offer, what He sees in you, and choose to hear His voice. **When no one thinks you are special or exceptional, God does.**

He did not put us here, at this time, to let trivial things or insecurities quiet our voices or silence our testimonies. We are each destined for so much more.

It is time to embrace our whole selves, every inch that God lovingly created and pronounced as good. We must practice gratitude for, and get comfortable with, the remarkable bodies that house our even more remarkable spirits. It is time to start seeing ourselves as He sees us: whole, complete, and perfect. Lumps, bumps, and all.

Exercise #1

How much energy do you spend focused on your outward self? Redirect a portion of that to build up the inner you.

_____

_____

_____

_____

_____

Exercise #2

What worldly practices or influences can you cut out of your life? Try replacing one or two of them this week with something that reaffirms your worth.

_____

_____

_____

_____

_____

My weaknesses give me the opportunity to invite God into my life.

CHAPTER 5

The Race For Holiness

I remember coming home from church one Sunday feeling a bit discouraged. My congregation is chock-full of spiritual giants. We have women with unshakable faith, love of the scriptures, and dedication to family history and temple attendance. As they share their thoughts, testimonies, and experiences, living the gospel seems so easy, so natural for them.

After a women's meeting, I found myself spiraling, wondering, "Why don't *I* get lost in my scriptures and have a hard time putting them down? Why don't *I* want to spend all my date nights in the temple? Why do *I* get bored by family history? Why do *I* still have gospel questions when everyone else seems to believe so easily?"

One afternoon, I shared these frustrations with my husband as I longed for different spiritual gifts. I thought I would be more valuable to God if I were more like the women I so looked up to.

As I was bemoaning my lack of traditional spirituality to him, he turned to me and said, "Are you kidding me?" He then went on to share the spiritual gifts he sees in me and how grateful he is for them. **I suddenly realized that by focusing on only the strengths of others, I had completely forgotten about what the Lord had blessed me with.** In that moment, Mike's voice was the voice of the Spirit, and I believed what he saw in me. His words allowed me to shift my perspective and be grateful for the personal gifts I had been given instead of envious of what I was lacking.

As I continued to ponder that situation, a favorite scripture came to mind, Ether 12:27:

"And if men come unto me I will show unto them their weakness. I give unto men weakness that they may be humble; and my grace is sufficient for all men that humble themselves before me; for if they humble themselves before me, and have faith in me, then will I make weak things become strong unto them."

As I digested those inspiring words, a light went on. **Our Heavenly Father GIVES us our weaknesses; they are a gift from Him and part of HIS plan**, not just some human defect I have to endure. He chose my weaknesses, especially for me, so I can be humble, turn to Him, and, if I am willing, turn them into strengths. **My weaknesses don't diminish my worth; they are part of it**. So, instead of wallowing in what I am not spiritually, **I can see my weakness as an opportunity to invite God into my life.**

This is where I love inserting the word YET into my thought processes. Maybe I don't love the scriptures all the time YET. Maybe I don't want to spend eight hours in the temple YET. Maybe I haven't caught the spirit of Elijah YET. Maybe I am not as faithful as I want to be YET.

But, **I have infinite worth in this imperfect state**, and one day I can become the woman I would so like to be and the woman God intends me to be— IF I turn to Him. Surely you have your own spiritual weaknesses, your own struggles, but remember that they were chosen for you. Will you use them to invite God into your life and connect with Him in a way you never have before? How will you use them to become stronger, brighter, and more of the woman God intends you to be? How will they help you connect with others who have similar struggles or spiritual challenges?

When I was asked by Deseret Book to speak at "Time Out for Women," I was shocked and humbled by the opportunity. I am so far from the spiritual giants they normally choose to engage and inspire rooms full of women. But I was determined to share myself, my struggles, and my testimony in a way that might touch those who came to listen.

As I prepared my talk, I felt an outpouring of the Spirit and was confident in the message God wanted me, a small and simple person, to share. I had prayed, fasted, practiced, and practiced some more. The night before my first presentation in Layton, Utah, I met the women and men I would be speaking with. They were well known, revered, influential, and inspiring. I felt a little out of place, but pushed through my insecurities because I had faith and trust in the message God had imprinted on my heart. Because of this, I was sure I could be a part of the inspired event the next day. I was calm and ready.

When Saturday morning came, I felt excitement and a healthy dose of nerves. Then, as I listened to each talk and heard the experiences each presenter shared, I began to feel like an imposter. Who was I to think I could ever be a part of this heavenly all-star lineup? I was nothing more than a regular old mom! I didn't teach institute or spend hours a day as a scholar of the scriptures. I hadn't written a book, didn't research Church history, hadn't been to the Holy Land, wasn't especially funny, and didn't have a YouTube channel people couldn't get enough of. What in the world was I doing there? How could I make a difference to the women who had come hoping for holy revelation?

As luck would have it, I was the last speaker of the day, and with each hour the doubts got stronger and harder to stifle. By 2:00 p.m., I was close to physically sick thinking about my upcoming moment under the bright lights. Then, a presenter I had only met the night before leaned over in the middle of someone else's talk and whispered out of the blue, "Just be yourself. That is why they asked you to be here."

Those two sentences changed everything for me. I could be myself. I could be the best, most authentic, faithful, prepared, and loving version of myself, and I could share the message God had whispered to me. My fear and doubt left me (though the nerves did not) and I was, once again, confident that I really was the one God needed that day.

I didn't give a flawless performance or get a standing ovation, but I know I touched hearts that snowy February afternoon, and I realized that **even when I doubt my own worth, God doesn't.**

When I think about a woman who is comfortable with her purpose and is divinely connected to God, my mind immediately goes to Marilee Killpack. I am in awe, not only of her miraculous story, but of the years of quiet, consistent effort that prepared her to embrace an impossible circumstance with complete faith and trust in her Father in Heaven.

Her son, Abram, was diagnosed with a rare, one-in-a-million, almost always terminal disease, and their family sacrificed everything for his shot to live. During this time, Marilee was given a blessing that said, "Your whole life has prepared you for this."

Truer words could not have been uttered. When you hear Marilee tell her story, it is obvious where she has always placed her focus, continually on her Savior. After spending time with her, I was in complete awe of her steadfast goodness.

This caused me to take stock of my own spirituality, and I panicked. There had been so many times I hadn't made the right choice, had been spiritually lazy, or chosen to not involve God. I was painfully humbled as I realized how far I had to go and felt almost completely defeated.

Holding onto a shred of hope, I asked Marilee the questions that were pounding on my heart: "What if something earth shattering happens, and you haven't prepared? What if you are in something deep but don't have those holy habits? What if you haven't taken the time to really know God? Then what? Where does that leave you?" She wisely replied:

"I would tell you to give it a shot. What do you have

to lose? Experiment on the word and see what fruit it yields. The word of God lets you find Jesus in the depths of your trials and allows you to connect with Him when there is no one else to turn to. He increases your capacity to think logically, gives you fresh perspective, and makes things much more clear. He was my lifeline. **If you are in deep, this is no time to give up on the Lord."**

With tears in my eyes, I caught my breath. He won't give up on me, and I won't give up on Him. I can start where I am, and I can experiment. And if I must, I can start over and over again. So, if you are feeling spiritually less than others, like your biology is too much to overcome, or like your growth is not coming as quickly as you wish it would, it's okay. **Good things take time. Growth takes time.** Have a little grace and patience with your own spiritual improvement, and never forget the word "yet."

Be yourself. Be the best version of it as often as you can. This is exactly who God needs you to be, nothing more, nothing less. He has placed inside you all of the goodness and inspiration you need to share with the world, so be brave, take that step into the dark, and bask in His light.

———

Exercise #1

Think about and write down two of your weaknesses. Invite your Heavenly Father into your life as you turn them into strengths.

_____

_____

_____

_____

_____

Exercise #2

On a scale of 1 to 10, how satisfied are you with your own spiritual growth right now? Think of one thing you can add to your life to help it increase (spend more time in the scriptures/attend an institute class/ watch a _Come, Follow Me_ study session/listen to a gospel podcast). Schedule time to make it happen.

_____

_____

_____

_____

_____

God wants us to understand who we really are, underneath it all.

CHAPTER 6

I Am More Than My Net Worth

I was born a planner. I knew exactly how I wanted my life to turn out, and for a while, reality played right into my plan. Mike and I had both graduated from college and landed great jobs in Washington, D.C. After a few years there, we bought a home in Arizona, where he got started in the booming commercial real estate industry. We had three boys, and life was going just swimmingly. We always had enough for us and enough to share. We were active in our congregation, had callings we loved, and enjoyed the ups and downs of a young family.

The market had been good for a while, so we took a leap of faith and put money down to build a big, new, beautiful home. It seemed like things couldn't get much better, and that we were being materially blessed for all our hard work in our personal, professional, and spiritual lives.

When the market crashed in 2008, we were completely blindsided. I will never forget the optimistic worry in my husband's voice as we discussed what was next. His job was 100% commission, and Arizona was hit hard. We had just put much of our savings down on a house, and with no money coming in, life was about to get very difficult and more real than either one of us had ever experienced. I went from girls' lunches and mall shopping to coupon clipping and food-storage living. No more coordinated outfits, no more fabulous date nights; everything came to a screeching halt, and we were left wondering, "What do we do now?"

Our prayers were fervent, pleading. We begged for help, guidance, a way out, but nothing came. This was life, chance, and choice. There would be no quick fix, no Hail Mary, no winning lottery ticket to wipe the struggle away. Our Heavenly Father had something else in mind. His end goal was not for us to be a well-dressed family in a perfectly-curated home. No, He wanted us to grow and change; He wanted us to learn humility and grace; **He wanted us to understand who we really were, underneath it all.**

After a year of trying to make things work, we backed out of our dream home and sold the house we lived in. We waded through difficult financial decisions and agonized over our perfect life, now changing course. We uprooted our family so Mike could attend graduate school in Michigan, where we lived with our three kids in drab student housing.

But what we found there, in between those gray skies, long winters, and never-enough dollars, was light. Our community quickly embraced us and taught us more about openness, generosity, and true charity than we had ever known before. They accepted us immediately, 20 of them waiting on the curb in the rain for us to arrive. They took our kids to play and unloaded our moving van with warm smiles. They delivered a basket of essentials on our first night and had us over for breakfast the next morning, though none of them truly had extra to spare. Never had I seen such genuine selflessness and acceptance. It felt like Zion.

As we lived together for the next two years, our Michigan friends taught me that you don't need a certain amount of square footage to invite someone into your life and that goodness has nothing to do with the size of your house or the balance of your bank account and everything to do with your heart.

They helped me see money for what it really is: neutral. There is nothing inherently good or inherently bad about it, but our attitude toward it, the importance we assign it, and the way it dictates how we feel about ourselves and others can distort our vision if we aren't careful.

Is it a sin to not have enough? To make a bad financial choice? To need help or assistance for a time? No. Should you feel badly about doing well? Having extra or prospering? Of course not. Is the person who earns less per year seen as less-than by God? Not at all. Does God reward His favorites with extra cash? Obviously not. Does He expect us to be wise stewards of what we have and unselfish towards those in need no matter what? YES!

A few years ago, my social media feed was full of accounts that prompted me to buy things or made me feel like my abundant life was lacking because I didn't wear the latest fashion, decorate with the most up-to-date trends, or spend my time in the most luxurious places. I constantly felt envious and empty because **when we search for our worth in material things of no consequence, we will find exactly that: nothing of consequence.**

I decided I needed an intentional break from consumerism. I cleaned out every account that, on a regular basis, made me feel like I needed to purchase something to be fulfilled. Then, I unfollowed every person or business that made me feel like my life, and what I had, was not good enough.

I realized that I could go back to those sites any time I needed a gift idea, fashion advice, or a new couch; they would still be there! But I did not need to invite them into my life on a daily basis; I could visit them on *my* terms, when I actually had a need. That Exercise was so freeing. I felt an immediate shift in my brain and was exponentially more content with the happy life I was leading. I stopped worrying about the next best thing and started appreciating the things I already had. Most importantly, I had time to understand who the Giver of all gifts is and how much He loves me for exactly who I am.

This knowledge is invaluable and changes who we are. When we internalize it, we become people who share what we have, who pursue purpose instead of pleasure, who self-reflect and generously give. We begin to believe in the law of abundance and know that there really is enough for everyone, and no need to hoard possessions, time, or talents.

We start seeing our success, not as our own doing, but as a combination of the talents God has blessed us with, connections we are fortunate to have, simple luck, good timing, *and* hard work. We become comfortable acknowledging the advantages that helped get us to where we are, give credit to the people that have contributed to our success, and look for ways to offer a leg up to others who might not have been afforded the same privileges. We stop saying we did it all on our own or boasting about our incredible work ethic, and realize that it has always been about so much more than that. Instead, we give God all the glory and live like we really believe it.

When this change of heart happens, sharing becomes natural because we understand that nothing we have was ever really ours to begin with. There is no more judgement of others' financial choices, lack of affluence, or incredible wealth, and instead time is spent figuring out how life can be more equitable for everyone. People start taking precedence over things. There is contentment when there used to never be enough, and focus is moved from the almighty dollar to the true Almighty.

This is what prosperity really is: Knowing you are right with God, which allows you to live in eternal abundance.

———————

Exercise #1

Write out every material blessing you have been given recently. Tonight, take the time to name some or all of them individually in your prayer.

_____

_____

_____

_____

Exercise #2

Think of the people who have been most influential in your life. Notice their different financial situations and realize the good each of them have accomplished with varied means. Try to remember that lesson in your own life.

_____

_____

_____

_____

Let go of judgement. Walk arm in arm. Stop the stones.

CHAPTER 7

Let's Be
Stone-Catchers

There was a time I had motherhood all figured out.
Well, figured out for everyone else. I sat on my park
bench and quietly judged. Parents were letting too
many things go, especially TV shows and bedtime.
They didn't play with their kids enough and dele-
gated "Duck, Duck, Goose" to older siblings. They
didn't pack bags full of healthy snacks in case of
hunger or boredom, pay attention to the newest research on how to do everything "right," or correct
the appalling words I kept hearing their children use.

Then, my two young kids became four older ones,
and we entered a new stage. All of a sudden I had
turned into the type of mom I wondered about; the
one I quietly (and sometimes not-so-quietly) cri-
tiqued; the one I tried to give pointers to. When my
boys were eleven, nine, eight, and three, I wrote the
following in an article addressed to my former self:

My three-year-old rarely watches TV, but when
he does it is *not* PBS. He watches shows with his

57

brothers who are pretty into *Star Wars*, *Chopped*, and action movies, like *Spider-Man*. He doesn't go to bed until about 10 pm. It works for us. He is still happy, silly, and easy to be around, and we love our crazy nights with each other.

I used to go to the park to play with my kids, but now, I go to the park to give us all some social time away from each other. They no longer get to interrupt me to fulfill their every whim. For too long, I was at their beck and call at all hours, and I thought this made me a great mother. It took years to realize that it actually made me an exhausted mother with very needy children.

I no longer carry a diaper bag or snacks. I don't have a strategy for every obstacle we encounter, and my youngest held onto bottles and pacifiers way longer than I care to admit. We've loosened up about language and frequently hear potty talk.

I am now on the other side of my former parenting fence, and I'm eating my words . . . funny how often that happens as a mother. Now I'm the one hoping new friends don't decide to cancel a playdate after hearing that lunch was nachos and fruit snacks.
I wish I would have climbed off my own high horse when my kids were younger. I should have looked for the good, appreciated the differences, learned from seasoned examples, and anticipated the need

for a few extra Goldfish at the park.

Re-reading and remembering those moments brings a smile to my face. You would think that with such a profound realization, I would have learned my lesson, and never criticize again, but strangely, I still went on judging the next stage of mothers just a bit, and much more quietly, but certain *I* would do things "right." I wondered why parents didn't require respect from their teenagers or why they allowed certain kids to sleep so late they wasted an entire day. It baffled me when teens didn't attend church or youth group activities or have respectable hair. I couldn't believe the way some kids were allowed to dress, the grades they brought home, or the stupid things their parents tolerated for fun. I was sure my kids would never be like that as I efficiently solved all their problems from the outside.

Then, I had my own teenagers, and **I started to understand the value of picking your battles and preserving relationships**. I learned that hair means nothing, and natural consequences are incredibly painful but necessary for true growth. I realized that it is healthy to let go of some control and allow teens to figure things out without a dictator on their shoulder or a puppet master behind the scenes, even if it means a rockier road.

If only I could apologize and ask forgiveness for mindlessly judging. If only I could put my arms around every parent and let them know, "I get it now." What if I saw their efforts and, more importantly, their children, through God's eyes?

These lessons have the incredible ability to refine our spirits. I have learned something essential about my own worth as I have stopped questioning and judging others. I have come to understand God's infinite love for us. He loves us through the testy attitudes, resistance, rebellion, and bad hair. He sees my potential and wants me to reach it, but He is also willing to be patient, to sit and abide with me as I figure it all out, sometimes through ugly and painful life lessons.

When my kids mess up, make me miserable, or test me to the point of what feels like no return, the capacity of my love miraculously continues to increase, to bear more than I thought I was capable of, and to cheer louder and harder for them than I ever thought possible. I know who they can become, and I will wait and watch and love until they get there. I am working on feeling this same way for all those in my life, because this is the example our Heavenly Father set for us. **When we put aside judgment and instead walk arm in arm together, everything changes**.

One afternoon I was at the pool with a friend. We watched as a very fit mom in a sporty two-piece with chiseled arms, visible abs, and perfectly-toned legs walked by. We looked at each other knowingly, silently thinking the same thing: "Must be nice to be so genetically blessed" or "How lucky is she to have enough time and money to get a body like that."

Then we saw her go to the side of the pool and lift a very heavy child with severe special needs out of the water, wrap her in a towel, and lovingly carry her back to their blankets and chairs.

We looked at each other guiltily, embarrassingly put in our place for our quick judgments. You see, in order to take care of her daughter, she needed a body like that, one that was strong and healthy. Those muscles weren't there to flaunt; they served a crucial purpose. She didn't get them the easy way or most likely even the fun way; she earned every single ripple on her body through selfless love and service.

It made me realize how easy it is to look on the outside, on the filtered photo, on the Sunday best, and assume I know what is going on in the lives of others, when who they are is so much deeper than most of us are willing to discover. It is easy to dismiss people because they seem to have it all, but those who are spiritually, physically, socially, or emotionally great have most likely paid a price to get there. **How often I want things the quick and easy way! I want the muscles without the lifting; I want**

the humility without the heartache; I want the empathy without the suffering. But that is not the plan. Those who are this way have paid the price.

At my grandmother's funeral, my uncle told of a time when he couldn't wait to share a juicy bit of neighborhood gossip with his mom. Her immediate response was, "People who live in glass houses don't throw stones." His little boy heart was hoping for a much better reaction to the titillating information he had to share, so he tried once more. Again he heard, "People who live in glass houses don't throw stones."

This same message occurs in the New Testament when Jesus halted the condemnation of the woman taken in adultery by saying, "He that is without sin among you, let him first cast a stone at her" (John 8:7). He stopped the stones.

Bryan Stevenson, an attorney-turned-activist who started substantial prison reform in the US and authored the powerful book *Just Mercy*, asks his readers to not just refrain from throwing stones but to become stone-catchers: people who will stand up for those under fire and protect those who are too beaten down to defend themselves. There have been so many incredible examples of stone-catchers in my life.

I encountered a stone-catcher years ago in the aisles

of Target. I was trying to reason with my unreasonable two-year-old while I held a screaming baby. Just before I lost it all, a woman said to me, "I love how you speak so kindly to your children even when they are giving you a hard time. You are a wonderful mother." I was saved by a stone-catcher.

My friend Jessica had just delivered her sixth baby and was barely staying afloat. At the time, her third-grader was diagnosed with ADD, was struggling in school, and Jessica didn't have the bandwidth to help him. His teacher rescued them both. She took that little boy under her wing without complaint, loved him, taught him, and ensured his academic success all year, never once questioning Jessica's lack of involvement or choice to have another baby when her plate seemed so full. She carried them both through that year when it would have been so easy to do the opposite.

A few years ago, my friend MJ was going through a divorce she never expected. She braced herself for whispers, judgments, and isolation, but instead found hope and strength in her family and friends. They were her stone-catchers. They offered couches to sleep on so she didn't have to spend the nights alone, and listening ears when she couldn't take the heartbreak.

One afternoon, my grandfather asked my cousin to

help him put up a welcome-home sign on the gate that marks the entrance to their polished, private community. As they were tying it to the fence, my cousin asked where the man was returning from, assuming it would be from military service, college, or a mission. He was startled at the answer: "He is coming home from prison, and I want him to know that we are happy he is back with us."

That day, my grandfather stood proudly and caught this man's stones so he could walk back into life knowing that someone was on his side, someone was rooting for him, someone was glad he was home.

Stone-catching happens constantly in my own ward, where people leave judgment behind and instead focus on love. It happens during sacrament meeting when an early returned missionary is greeted with happy hugs and hellos instead of embarrassed avoidance.

It happens in Relief Society as sisters share struggles openly. I remember one lesson about the Sabbath Day when many women talked about the added joy in their home when they cut out media. One single mom of teens said, "I have tried this and there has never been a worse Sunday for my family." The space felt safe enough for honesty because it is a place where stones are caught, not thrown. Immediately a variety of ideas, perspectives, and supportive words were shared that were helpful and inclusive.

It was seen again when a sister admitted to struggling with the temple and was met with kind and open answers and a visit from a sister who has a passion for temple work, who wondered if she could answer any questions.

It happens in Young Men's when the distractor is brought into the fold, and the kid who hates church still really likes his leaders. It happens in Young Women's when advisors see daughters of Heavenly Parents instead of hemlines. It happens in Primary when the songs are so powerful and the doctrine is so pure that even the most unruly can't help but pause to feel the Spirit.

Stone catching happens when racism is discussed openly and neighbors and friends are willing to learn instead of get defensive, or when decades-old traditions and phrases are traded in for new language and activities that honor a variety of life experiences.

Of course, nothing is perfect. There are differences of opinion and those who have offended and been offended. There are kids who don't get along and those who feel on the fringe. But it is incredible what happens when we choose to see the worth of others through God's eyes. Not only are our hearts changed toward them, but toward ourselves as we understand how deep Christ reaches: to every ugly corner of our own soul. This allows us to hope for something better for ourselves, for those we love, and for strangers we have yet to encounter. It propels us to be agents of change.

During a "Time Out for Women" Q&A in Riverside, California, a difficult question was asked. The gist was, "My husband is struggling with a pornography addiction and I am struggling because of it. How can I love him through this?"

The room was silent, as that situation is heart wrenching and perhaps too familiar for too many. There were some practical answers about help and counseling and plenty of love and encouragement. Then I felt prompted to say,

Try seeing him as your son instead of as your husband. Try to picture how you would act if it was your son struggling . . . how you would help him, pray with him, love him, and hope for him. How you would do anything for him to heal, and how you would hope others would treat him during the process. Then try to do that for your husband. I know it isn't easy at all, but maybe shifting that perspective can give you hope and strength during the darkest times. Maybe you could try, for a time, to be his stone-catcher.

What might our world be like if we all committed to this cause? Can we smile at that teenager with wild friends and loud music and get to know him instead of rolling our eyes? Can we talk less about the schoolyard bully and invite her to play? Can we listen to people who are marginalized and figure out how to be an ally? Can we personally discuss differing ideas with each other instead of publicly calling people out? Can we rescue the mother who is barely holding on? Can we hold back our words of contempt and our defensive comments on the Internet and seek to understand first?

I have seen glimpses of this kind of world. I have been loved by people who see me instead of my faults, who see divine potential in my misbehaving children, who love unconditionally.

Through these types of people and my own humbling learning experiences, I think I am finally starting to appreciate worth through the eyes of God. **I am beginning to understand why He is willing to reach lower, cheer louder, and work harder for us than we ever really deserve.** Because He loves us, He gives us that true, undiluted love and is trusting us to give others the same.

Exercise #1

The next time you have the urge to judge someone, visualize yourself as their stone-catcher. See if you can stop your own judgments and change your habits.

_____

_____

_____

_____

_____

Exercise #2

When has someone held back their judgment of you or someone you love? Share that story and what it meant to you with a friend or group of women.

_____

_____

_____

_____

_____

You don't have to be everything. You just have to be yourself.

CHAPTER 8

Productivity Does Not Equal Progression

Have you ever known a generation as obsessed with productivity as ours is? Everywhere I look, the world is screaming about self-improvement, doing more with less, filling every second, achieving, achieving, achieving. There are a million book titles promising success and more of everything.

On the surface it sounds motivational, good, and true, but also exhausting. In an era where everyone has a side hustle, a passion project, and a non-profit, what happens if you are content with something more simple, less flashy, a little quieter?

When we moved to Michigan for graduate school with three kids and nothing left in the bank, I met Jenny. She was the one who took my kids as we pulled up to the curb and then later dropped off the basket of essentials on our first night.

When we walked into her tiny, little home for breakfast, nothing was perfect. Everything was old and handed down. The house was clean but cluttered with life and food and children. Each of her boys was in mismatched clothing that was either too big or too small. And it all felt amazing. She wasn't embarrassed or apologetic. She loved who she was and who her boys were. As she moved a stack of books for us to sit down, she really got to know us. No pretense. Just love.

We had never met before, but she shared her struggles and hopes and dreams with me as the wife of a PhD student, and let me share my fears with her. Her door and her heart were always wide open for a friend or a stranger. Her guard was down. Her kids were a happy sort of wild as she allowed them to explore the world, constantly in amazement over what they would find and what they could learn. There was no concern for germs, injuries, or danger because she was okay with natural occurrences, and she accepted life and the totality of the experience.

She loved having her kids be part of her world. She allowed them to cook and clean with her, which often resulted in crazy messes or cut fingers, and she let them create on their own terms. She once took me to a recycle shop to buy junk that our kids could then dump out all over her floor and hot-glue together into whatever their minds imagined. I thought she was crazy to allow that kind of mess and to live life without an agenda, but really, she just knew how to make the most of each day.

She was never in a hurry and always had room for a friend or stranger at her dinner or lunch table, no notice necessary. She didn't have much but always seemed to have plenty to share.

She taught me a different form of success than our world today touts. **She felt no pressure to be everything, but was so comfortable being herself** and magnifying her life and role in a way that she knew was right for her.

Her influence changed me. She changed the way I mothered, what I expected of myself and others, and she showed me the joys that come from just being—being there for your children, your husband, your friends, in a way that makes them feel so loved and important that no one would ever question their worth in your presence. To me, that is the ultimate definition of success. Jenny's life wasn't quiet or smooth, but it was intentional which was just the example I needed, since I often felt the push to do it all.

During one season of life, when I had crying babies at home, I honestly thought I would never sleep through the night again or have one minute to myself.

Doing just about anything felt overwhelming, and I know it sounds dramatic, but I thought that feeling would last forever. I felt constantly guilty about all I couldn't accomplish. I vividly remember, during that time, a stake president challenging our stake to attend the temple once a week. The temple was about 25 minutes away, I had a nursing baby, two other young boys, and a husband who worked long hours. He jumped on the obedience train and got up extra early every Friday to make the temple happen and offered me the same opportunity on another day, but I just couldn't. Instead, I sat home and felt guilty about my lack of spirituality, determination, and resolve.

Until one day, the spirit affirmed that I was exactly where I was supposed to be doing exactly what I needed to be doing. The temple suggestion was a great one for so many, but MY purpose during that season was different and just as necessary. I was more needed at home than I was in the temple and that was okay. It was confirmed to me that there would be many years when more frequent temple service would be a possibility, and a weight lifted. **Though I felt small and insignificant in so many ways during those years, I was reminded that God really does know me. He knows there are many wonderful and worthy things to be a part of, but He will lead me to the BEST things, for me and my family, if I turn to**

Him.

As life changes, the way He needs us changes. It can be difficult to be patient through parts of it, but I am forever grateful that Jenny taught me to embrace and engage in my current stage of life instead of wish it away. Nothing, not even the best or worst of times, is meant to last forever. My purpose one year might be to hang out at the park with friends, read books to my babies, and make dinner for my family. Another year it might be to spend hours in the schools, get involved in my community, and be the team mom. Later it might be to write a book, work full time, serve a mission, or be the world's best neighbor. Seasons of life are evidence of God's love, His willingness to let us grow, change, and become in all kinds of exciting and sometimes trial-filled ways. **Staying in tune with Him and listening for His Spirit helps me know when to push, when to slow down, when to be content, and when to reach for more.**

There is great importance in finding satisfaction but not perfection in our current phase of life. We can look for growth opportunities and carefully evaluate what will bring us closer to the woman God intends us to be, but also be okay to pause or change course when prompted to do so.

Our hyper-productive culture, the one that makes

us feel frantic and like we are always missing out on something bigger or better, does, at times, have me worried. What happens in a world where each person is so focused on themselves, their output, and their worldly, personal fulfillment that there is no room for the unplanned or unproductive? What if there is no time to stop and talk, volunteer to help, be quiet and introspective, or look out for one another? Is there a chance that in all this exceptional time management and even essentialism, that we are missing out on the moments that solidify who we really are?

One moment this year reminded me that we cannot lose sight of why we are here: to help others feel God's love.

A year and a half ago, I was in a really rough spot. I was going through some parenting stuff that consumed my mind, body, and spirit. One day, after dropping my kids at school, I sat in a parking lot praying, crying, and searching for answers. It was the out-loud kind of cry, the shake-your-whole-body kind of cry, the kind of cry that comes with words hurled to heaven. I really wanted the Lord to just fix things for me, maybe wave a magic wand or something, but I have enough experience to know that isn't the way things work. So instead, I begged Him to please send me someone I could talk to who would understand. My verbal, social self at least needed to talk it out.

After that good cry and fervent prayer, I felt composed enough to pull myself together and make it to a meeting I had planned on attending. It seemed insignificant and unnecessary at the moment, but I couldn't shake the idea that I needed to be there. At the very least it might be a nice distraction.

Right before the meeting started, I saw a friend who I am not especially close to but always enjoy conversing with, slip into the back row. She smiled and waved from the corner of the room, and it felt good to see a friendly face.

After the meeting, I stopped to ask the presenters a few questions and was pleasantly surprised to see this same friend waiting by the door. We caught up on the superficial parts of life, but when she asked me how things were really going, I opened all the way up. She felt safe, like an answer to a prayer, and I hoped she might understand and offer me a little comfort.

She listened without judgment, empathized, and shared her umbrella as we talked in the rain. She helped me sort things out and let me ramble and worry. She didn't offer a solution or mitigate my feelings. She didn't share something harder she had been through, but she did assure me that, eventually, everything would be okay. And for the first time in a while, I believed it.

I am sure I held her up for far too long, but she never once looked at her watch or pulled out her phone or tried to duck out before I was finished. She stood with me for as long as I needed, until I really did have to go. As I walked to my car, I felt a weight had been lifted. My situation hadn't changed, but she had taken a portion of my worry and anxiety and carried it with her, freeing a piece of me. The rest of the day felt different, a little more hopeful. How might I have felt if she hadn't stopped, if she was too busy to listen to the Spirit or to me?

I didn't expect any more from her—she gave me so much in that moment on the sidewalk—but her ministering wasn't over. That evening, she called and asked for my address because she wanted to bring me something. Normally I would refuse, hating that I had already monopolized so much of her time, but a part of me still craved that extra support, to know that I was not forgotten. So, instead of saying no, I said yes, grateful for the chance to see her again. She came to my door with a hot, delicious loaf of French bread, a smile, and a sincere note full of kind things she had noticed about me over the last couple of years. She had no idea how badly I needed that sustenance in every way. The bread and her note reminded me of the goodness in the world and inside of me.

She told me that she just wanted to check in and make

sure I was feeling better, but she also wanted me to know that it wasn't just chance that we crossed paths that afternoon. She had had no intention of being at the meeting, but had an overwhelming feeling that she needed to go. It seemed like a silly prompting, but she followed it, and I will be forever grateful that she did. God had sent her there just for me, to let me know that my prayers had not stopped at the ceiling of my minivan that morning, but they had reached Him. And He had sent someone running. He heard me. He understood me. And He would not leave me comfortless.

My sweet friend was an example of so many gospel truths that day:

- When someone needs us, we must take the opportunity to show up and slow down.

- Our time and our lives are not our own.

- We might have to take a detour in our perfectly-planned day if we want to fulfill a bigger, more meaningful purpose.

- We don't have to be family, neighbors, or best friends to make a difference.

- Nothing is more important than a brother or sister in need.

We cannot just be the people who check the "I cared about someone today" box and move along to better, more interesting scenes or let someone share their heart and soul, then dismiss them and their situation as if everything will be fine. We have to follow up. Following up shows investment, trust, and true Christlike charity. **We can never forget that WE are all the Lord has to fulfill His work of succoring, comforting, and loving**.

But, how can we lighten one another's loads if we never know they exist? If you are hurting or struggling or bearing a burden that is heavier than you can manage, open up and share your heart with someone you trust. There is no weakness in accepting help, and people are often so much better than we give them credit for. Take a chance, and remember that it is okay to need. Needing unites us and bonds us in ways nothing else can, so embrace that feeling and give someone the opportunity to truly minister to you. Through that process, you will get a glimpse of Christ's love and have the strength to turn around and pass that love along.

If we want to be truly fulfilled, we must **leave open spaces in our day and in our hearts. Our lives cannot be so full that the most important work, the truly worthwhile moments, are lost in the clutter of the unimportant.**

Exercise #1

Look at your next week and free up time every day for a divine detour. Pencil in "open" hours where you allow your life and heart to be where God needs them to be.

_____

_____

_____

_____

Exercise #2

Tonight, pray and ask God what your purpose is. Stop to listen and make small notes throughout the week as your inspiration becomes more clear.

_____

_____

_____

_____

There is strength, not shame, in struggle.

CHAPTER 9

Constantly Connected Always Lonely

When the world became digital, I noticed more and more women who were virtually connected to thousands of people, yet always lonely. They put on a happy, filtered face but were desperately wanting for more love, understanding, and real-life connection. I observed the same phenomenon with women who had plenty of online accounts and podcasts to keep them company but were missing something crucial in their everyday life. We need real, personal, honest connection. I once learned this lesson clearly but unfortunately just a little too late.

About six years ago, I lost a friend. She was a young, widowed mother of two, working full time to provide a life for her son and daughter. She was kind and energetic. She was happy and involved. We chatted as we picked up our boys from each other's houses and exchanged greetings over the back fence. She took my son to the splash pad, and I had hers over for movie night. She was a good mom who loved her kids.

But suddenly, one night, she was gone, and I was left wondering: Did she know I was her friend?

I was planning on getting closer to her. I wanted to have her family over for dinner. I thought about stopping by one day to help clean up the house. I meant to ask if I could take her kids so she could have a night off. Once life was a little less busy, I was going to really get to know her. But my best intentions were all too late.

I hope she had close friends, that she wasn't lonely, that someone knew about her health problems. It is incredible that in a world crammed full of people and buzzing with social media, so many of us don't really know each other. I really wanted to be her friend; I was planning on it, I just hadn't gotten around to it, and then she died without warning, leaving two young children wondering what would happen next.

After her death, **I decided that being friendly is just not enough. Being a real friend is what matters.** We need to know each other. We need to care. We need to love. We need to include and invite. Not everyone has a mother or sister or best friend. Sometimes friendship is not easy. Sometimes relationships take work. Sometimes outgoing people are friendless. Sometimes we just wish someone would realize how lonely we really are.

It is time to be a real friend. Real friends call on birthdays and stop by just to say hello. Real friends watch out for your children and have your back when no one else will. Real friends do what is inconvenient, make time for you, cry with you, and want the best for you. Real friends watch you make mistakes and forgive you because they know you, really know you, and they love you anyway.

That is who I should have been for her. It may not have made a difference in the way things ended, but it may have made the days before that a little brighter, a little less difficult, and a little less lonely. She may have had one more person in her corner. I could have been that person.

After that shocking day, I was left wondering, "What was so important that I hadn't made time for her? A load of laundry? A soccer carpool? An email?" It all seemed so frivolous as I watched her two children all alone.

I can't erase that day, but I can be better. We all can. **We must stop just "doing what we are supposed to do" and start truly caring for and loving each other**. It's more than a quick plate of cookies or a smile and a wave. It's taking the time to care.

That day, I promised to change: to find energy even when it felt like I was running on empty, to listen when I wanted to talk, and to pray for more strength when mine was gone. I would re-teach myself how to be a friend, even to those who might be different, needy, or closed, and I would find joy in the process of loving, serving, and connecting with them. Through that connection, I would begin to understand true worth in the sight of God.

If the question, "Did she know I was her friend?" ever arose again, I would be able to say with confidence, "Of course, she knew. We were wonderful friends."

For quite a few years, I held to this life motto. I took connection seriously and saw my life and heart open up in ways I never expected. My confidence increased, not because I had more friends, but because I was conscientiously choosing to be where God needed me most and opening my life to so many people who enriched it in all kinds of wonderful ways.

But then, life changed. My kids got older. I started to work more, and I didn't need people like I previously had. Connection was still important, but I had finally lived in a place long enough to be comfortable, and it felt so good to not have to try so hard. I basked in just having friends and being part of a group for the first time in what felt like forever. Then, again, an experience changed me.

I was invited to a fabulous party with delicious food and lovely company. I looked forward to an afternoon of meeting new people and reconnecting with old friends. I have taught myself to be a pretty outgoing person, even though it has not always come naturally, but as I walked in late and alone to that party and recognized only a handful of women, I was unusually nervous. I chatted with the three people I did casually know but didn't want to monopolize their time, so I looked for a place to sit and eat.

I bravely sat in an open chair and introduced myself to those I didn't know. We talked for a bit, but they all had to leave quickly to pick up kids from school, so I was left alone. I looked around for another spot, but the tables were full, so I sat by myself for too many painful minutes. Not one person looked up and noticed.

I was unprepared for how awkward and lonely I felt. I went from a confident 39-year-old woman back to an insecure 13-year-old girl in a matter of seconds, questioning if I was good enough to be at that kind of party. That horrible, cast-out feeling roared inside me until I couldn't stand it for one more minute, so I gathered my things to go.

That experience made it painfully obvious that the feeling of being unwanted doesn't end just because we grow up. We all want to belong, but so many men and women still feel lonely much of the time. They try but fail at friendship, watch from the outside, and still can't find a seat at the table. As followers of Christ, this shouldn't happen on our watch. **There should always be room in our pew, on our row, in our circle.**

Marjorie Pay Hinckley put it so well when she said:

> We are all in this together. We need each other. Oh, how we need each other. Those of us who are old need you who are young. And, hopefully, you who are young need some of us who are old. It is a sociological fact that women need women. We need deep and satisfying and loyal friendships with each other. These friendships are a necessary source of sustenance. We need to renew our faith every day. We need to lock arms and help build the kingdom so that it will roll forth and fill the whole earth[3]

My heart breaks wondering how many people have stopped attending church, not because of doctrine, but because they can't stand the idea of worshipping alone. How many neighbors feel snubbed because they don't fit in? How many new friendships have been overlooked because our church family gives us all the social experiences we need?

---

3 Pearce, Virginia H. *Glimpses into the Life and Heart of Marjorie Pay Hinckley. (Salt Lake City: Deseret Book, 1999), 254-255.*

That moment alone at the table reminded me to stop being so comfortable in the relationships I already have and to look out for and reach out to the one who might need me, even if she is 20 years older, speaks a different language, or is in an unfamiliar stage of life. **Godlike friendship should have no screening processes or prerequisites, it's just about who needs us most**.

We must be the women who introduce themselves to the new girls, who scoot over to make room, who make their circle a horseshoe. If we choose to open our eyes, there is probably always someone who is desperate for a friend, or even just a little connection.

Yes, there are a million valid excuses we can use to justify why we don't reach out. We are too shy, too busy, too different, too tired, too content, or too weighed down by our own mess. **But I am asking all of us, as disciples of Christ, to put the excuses away, and try to figure out how we CAN follow our Savior's example and embrace one more.**

The solutions can be simple, though perhaps a little uncomfortable. It's saving a seat for someone who isn't your best friend. It's sharing a sincere compliment with a teen who you think is just trouble. It's following up with a neighbor who you know has experienced heartache. It's asking the new guy to join you for Saturday basketball. It's choosing not to sit alone at a soccer game, even if you prefer it. It's finding out why someone left the Church instead of assuming and avoiding. It's talking to the grocery checker instead of looking at your phone. It's insisting that the difficult kid gets invited to the party and then making sure he feels loved.

This way of life, this inclusivity, can become a habit if we let it. It might take a while, a few years, or even a lifetime, but **wouldn't it be wonderful to be known as the person who broke down barriers, abolished cliques, refused to judge, and made this world just a little softer, a little easier, a little more accepting for all of us?** It is important for us to realize the power we have in creating connection in our own lives and what that effort can do for others.

I believe that connection only comes through vulnerability and honesty. Being real is hard, but being real about important things is the hardest. I'm not talking about the once-every-six-months, bare-your-soul Instagram post about struggling with perfectionism, the funny story about your "naughty" child, or the tell-all photo confession about leaving your dishes all night in your sparkling farmhouse sink. I am talking about actual honesty, about things that matter.

Most of us try, with all the energy of body and soul,

to keep up appearances, to put on happy faces, and sweep everything unpleasant under the rug. It is basically second nature to pretend like everything is always fine. But let me ask, for what?

I am not advocating for a litany of complaints and negativity. We know the world is not served by people who only see or talk about the bad. But **real relationships are not built on superficial platitudes and glossy smiles.**

What if your friends knew that postpartum depression is a daily nightmare, or that you think your toddler might have autism?

What if your neighbor found out that your heart is broken because your daughter continues to be unkind or your adult son refuses to come around?

What if you told your extended family that you were having a hard time paying the bills or were really struggling with your faith?

What if you admitted to your teen that you made a parenting mistake, or acknowledged that you actually weren't a perfect parent to your adult children?

What if you simply admitted to not knowing everything or sincerely asked others for advice and then listened?

What if you told the truth? Not a confession for the world to see, a social media post, or a tirade about someone else's problem with you, but actual, real struggles shared with someone close to you who cares? What would happen if you opened your heart?

Do you think the people who supposedly love you would walk away? It shouldn't be that way. In fact, I am positive that **letting your guard down and being vulnerable almost always welcomes others in**. With the right people by your side, honesty will bring you solutions, empathy, real love, and friendship. It has happened this way countless times for me.

As a young mom with three little boys, I arrived at our neighborhood park at a complete breaking point. I could have pretended to be a rockstar and played hide-and-seek or pushed toddlers on the swings, but instead I was honest. My friends picked up the pieces of my lackluster motherhood moment and stepped right in, giving me a few minutes of sanity that I desperately needed.

When I share questions about my faith with fellow members of my congregation, there are no cold shoulders or dropped jaws. Instead there are quiet nods, helpful ideas, and words and examples of encouragement and validation. They don't need me to be a saint who regurgitates rehearsed answers; they love me because we are all imperfect together and are doing our best to figure it all out.

At the end of a gym class a few years ago, my tears were flowing after an especially hard week. A few caring women noticed, and I opened up. I was shocked as these women shared their own battles, some so painful that my petty problems were put in perspective. They inspired me to carry on with faith. They could have closed themselves off, preferring to remain the strong gym women I always thought they were, but instead they became so much more.

I think we forget that knowledge has the power to change hearts. After learning about a friend's depression, my capacity for love and patience with her increased, and I stopped expecting more than she could give. When another friend confided in me about her son's emotional and mental hardships, I was able to see him as a warrior instead of just a really hard kid. I became his biggest fan. **If you give the truth a try, I think people will surprise you**. **There is strength, not shame, in struggle.**

Let's stop trying to power through everything until it is too late. **No one should have to wait until they are completely broken before asking for help, love, or understanding.** Independence is often revered and celebrated, but it is also terribly lonely.

I have often wondered how we can be expected to bear one another's burdens if no one will share them or how we can mourn with those that mourn if everyone is too guarded to show their sadness. I don't think God sent us here in families, extended families, communities, and congregations so we could walk our most difficult roads alone.

We often bar ourselves off from divine intervention because of our own egotistical need or fear-based hesitation to let others see our weaknesses, but He is counting on us to intertwine our lives and become united in Him. It's time to let each other in.

———————

Exercise #1

Do you have enough meaningful connections in your life? Make a list of a few women you would like to get to know better, or call one immediately and plan time to be together.

_____

_____

_____

_____

_____

Exercise #2

If you are part of a group, invite one more to join you in your next outing. If you are not, put out an open invitation to connect, and see who is also looking for friendship.

_____

_____

_____

_____

_____

God can do so much more with us than we can do with ourselves.

CHAPTER 10

The Power Of Change

I remember talking to my teenage son one day when he was feeling down. He said that he thought he might be feeling depressed. We don't take mental health lightly, so I immediately wanted to know more. As we talked, he realized that he wasn't exercising much, and he wasn't taking the opportunity to be with friends or participate with the family. He had a long list of things that needed to be accomplished, but he was ignoring it, which was making him feel especially stressed. He wasn't praying or reading his scriptures consistently, and he was spending most of his time playing video games, watching YouTube, and just wasting time. Add on a lack of sleep and not enough healthy food, and life was looking pretty bleak.

As he verbalized his observations, we both kind of smiled. His actions and habits were basically a recipe for disaster. Those depressed feelings were a warning to him that he wasn't meeting the needs of his mind, body, or spirit, and he needed to make some changes.

He had gotten into a routine that had stunted his growth and progression.

As cruel as it seems, **lack of motivation and dissatisfaction are vital to our growth. When we feel those feelings, we are pushed to make necessary changes in our lives to better ourselves, to connect with the divine, and to rediscover the spark inside us.**

Moving from complacency to action can be so overwhelming, especially when we are stuck in a perfectionist mindset or an all-or-nothing spiral. As I write this book, we're in the midst of the Coronavirus pandemic. During the first three months of the quarantine, the lack of control I felt often immobilized me. I was either the world's greatest mother and belonged on the cover of *Quarantine Magazine* or a complete and utter failure. I rode this detrimental roller coaster daily, until some advice from my friend, Emily Orton, changed everything. She advised me to figure out what makes me feel successful and joyful in motherhood, and do more of it. Then, when night came, instead of listing all the ways I fell short, I was to reflect on all the ways I found joy and success.

This process is helping me understand that no one can do things right all the time. I no longer let one bad exchange, too much screen time, my working hours, or forgotten chores cloud all the good stuff.

Perfection is not possible, and life is too short to constantly tally my failures.

I now make deliberate choices to make the best things, the things I love, happen as often as possible. I love getting outside, having one-on-one time with my kids, and staying up late to chat. I love reading together, talking about big ideas, and cheering from the sidelines. I love good food, sharing spiritual truths, and playing sports I am horrible at. I love getting in the water (if I haven't just washed my hair), hiking, and dancing just so my teens will roll their eyes. I love learning, serving, and praying together. When these good moments are going on, I try to be present, *really* present, so I don't miss them.

But, I don't do ALL of these things ALL day, or even ALL of these things EVERY day. I still work and clean and talk on the phone, but I also make sure at least one good thing happens every day. Then, I focus on those stellar motherhood moments, giving myself credit for the relationships I am nurturing and the memories we are making. Are there a million less-than-ideal times too? Of course, and I'm constantly trying to improve, but **life is too short to focus on failures when instead I can focus on joy.**

Sitting back and feeling satisfied with our progress is crucial to our growth, but there are also times when we need to troubleshoot, experiment, and dig into uncomfortable change. I am working on doing this without beating myself up before the process even begins. I am trying to be grateful for "divine discontent," which was introduced to me by Michelle Craig. She defines it this way:

> Divine discontent comes when we compare "what we *are* [to] what we have the power to *become*." Each of us, if we are honest, feels a gap between where and who we are, and where and who we want to become. We yearn for greater personal capacity. We have these feelings because we are daughters and sons of God, born with the Light of Christ, yet living in a fallen world. These feelings are God given and create an urgency to act.
>
> **We should welcome feelings of divine discontent that call us to a higher way.** [4]

Divine discontent is a good thing. We should embrace the desire to improve without first hating ourselves, becoming obsessive, or freezing with hopelessness. Instead, **we can consciously choose to change.** Last year, I felt this divine discontent in a funny way. I had been reading all about the benefits of hugs and touch, and I knew my family needed more of

---

4 Michelle D. Craig, *"Divine Discontent." Ensign, November 2018: https://www.churchofjesuschrist.org/study/general-conference/2018/10/divine-discontent?lang=eng*

it. When my kids were little, it was so easy, but the older and bigger they got, the less natural it seemed. So I did less and less of it—until I realized that my little and not-so-little boys needed more of that kind of love in their lives from me. I started working on things. I set reminders on my phone to hug my kids and made small efforts to put my arm around them or rub their backs when we sat next to each other. Eight second hugs became mandatory after prayers. I was surprised by how these small, intentional efforts started changing me, making me more aware of how crucial physical affection can be.

In the middle of this improvement, I found myself in Relief Society sitting next to a new woman in our ward. She was on the end, and I was right next to her. During one point in the lesson, she shared something really deep and personal. She started to weep and opened up her heart to all of us about an extremely touching experience. When she was finished, I knew I needed to do something to show her that she was accepted and loved in her new congregation. I leaned over and patted her knee, then froze. Who pats someone's knee when they are bearing their soul? Perhaps I hadn't come as far as I had hoped. As I watched her dry her eyes, the spirit said, "Brooke. She doesn't need a pat on her knee. She needs you to wrap your arms around her."

I didn't even know her! I'm not a hugger! It was going to be so weird! But I did it. I reached over and put my arms around her and whispered, "I am so awkward at this, but I wanted to give you a hug." We both laughed as she dried her eyes.

I had been working on myself and trying to change, so when the spirit pushed me out of my comfort zone into a place where I could be better for her and for myself, I was ready. That day, I was reminded that **God can do so much more with me than I can do with myself, and that who we become is an accumulation of small changes and our willingness to hear Him.**

It can be so easy to get caught up in who we already are, who we previously were, or who others think we are, instead of trying to improve or find a better way. Satan, the Father of Lies, tells us things like:

"You were just raised that way. There is nothing you can do about it."

"The world owes you more. People are trying to keep you down."

"You have never been good enough. Who is to say you are good enough now?"

"People treat you badly because you deserve it."

"You were born with anger issues. You've always had a hard time controlling your temper. Other people will just have to understand."

"Your marriage has always been difficult. It just is what it is."

"That's just your vice; everyone has one. It's not like it's a big deal."

"You don't have a part in this gospel; your story is too different. No one cares if you are here."

One of my all time favorite quotes is by Elder Hallstrom, who said,

When any of us conclude—"That's just the way I am," we give up our ability to change. We might as well raise the white flag, put down our weapons, concede the battle, and just surrender—any prospect of winning is lost. While some of us may think that does not describe us, perhaps every one of us demonstrates, by at least one or two bad habits, "That's just the way I am."

Well, we [are here tonight] because who we are is not who we can become. We meet here tonight in the name of Jesus Christ. We meet with the confidence that His Atonement gives every one of us—no matter our weaknesses, our frailties, our addictions—the ability to change. We meet with the hope that our future, no matter our history, can be better.[5]

How powerful is that? Our situations now do not have to remain the same. *We* do not have to remain the same. Just because this is the way we do things now, does not mean they have to stay that way.

Changing takes bravery. It is not easy to say, even as an adult, "No, I am not that person anymore." Change is uncomfortable for us and often for the people around us. If you have always been impatient, it is not easy to convince those you love that you are working on patience. If you have always nagged your spouse, it will take some time before he sees you as someone different. If you have had a hard time showing gratitude, it will take more than one thank-you note to be seen as a grateful person. If you have always loved juicy gossip or followed TV shows that glorify the world, it will take sheer willpower and prayer to stay away from both, and to find other commonalities with friends and family.

Changing is even harder when those closest to you want to keep you down. My friend, Jane (name has

---

5 Donald Hallstrom, "What Manner of Men," Ensign, May 2014: https://www.churchofjesuschrist.org/study/general-conference/2014/04/what-manner-of-men?lang=eng

been changed) lived through a nightmare when she realized her husband had been having an affair for over a year.

That act of betrayal had her consistently wondering what was wrong with her. She felt lost, unloved, and broken. After much prayer and soul searching, she decided to try and work things out with her husband, or at least be patient before making a final decision on divorce. That choice felt right but led to some of the most difficult years of her life as her husband be-littled her and blamed her for his choices and actions.

Jane remembers him pointing out her every flaw. She was too "goody-goody," didn't dress right, was too boring, didn't have a career, and was way too into their kids. He took the qualities she loved about herself and framed them in ways that were negative and demeaning. She tried to turn into the woman he wanted: she dressed differently, acted flirty, got interested in new topics, and focused more on him, but still nothing was good enough. One day, as he was telling her again about all the ways she fell short, she heard the words, "He's not seeing you right," straight from God. She said those words out loud to him and often to herself.

She had finally caught a much-needed glimpse of who she really was through the eyes of God and began the difficult mental and emotional work to analyze the lies and insecurities her husband had projected on her.

She took action. She started seeing a professional counselor and set reminders on her phone that said things like "Capable and Confident" or "Clear and Assertive" or "Self-defined and Independent." She made a list of the qualities she loved about herself and hung them in her closet so she was reminded of them daily. As she looked in the mirror, she would pray to see herself as God saw her. She got into running, made new friends, and went back to graduate school. As her affirming feelings started to grow, she was even more motivated to improve herself. Even in a desperate situation, she knew she was smart, capable, and loved.

As Jane tethered her life to her Savior, she was blessed with courage, a fresh perspective, and the fierceness to fight for her family. The days were excruciating and the nights endless, but today you would hardly recognize Jane. She is tough and humble and full of confidence. She knows who she is.

Yes, change is hard but also beautiful. My friends, it is time to push, to open our hearts, to restore ourselves to the women God knows we can be. We don't do this to impress others or tout our own righteousness, but because there is intense joy that comes from both the process and the outcome of change.

I remember a conversation I had with my husband 10 years ago. He was having a hard time being patient and said that it felt like he was taking three steps forward and two steps back. We came to the conclusion that a gain of one step is still moving in the right direction, even if he wished he was moving faster. Then, a few weeks ago, this happened:

We'd had a rough Sunday and our home was feeling quite contentious. The day was filled with unkind words, fights, sarcasm, intentional annoyance, short tempers, and downright rudeness. We had been in that spot before, but had made a concerted effort to make some big changes in our family, so those feelings were atypical, and I knew something needed to change.

I was frustrated, and my first thought was to give everyone a stern "talking to" about attitudes and gratitude and shaping up and getting it together. I rehearsed every power-packed, exclamatory sentence in my mind. It was good stuff. Biting. It would put them in their place.

But my husband had a better idea. All those years of working on patience, all those prayers for help, all those tiny steps forward had changed him. Instead of a tongue lashing, he gathered us for a family council and asked, one by one, if there was something bigger going on. I was shocked as they all willingly opened up.

One said school was stressful and his expectations were too high. He was overwhelmed, annoyed, and short tempered, and ended up in tears. We talked about time management and perfectionism. He agreed to let go a little and looked visibly lighter from the support and love.

Another said he was off because of too little to do. Work and sports had slowed down, so he had spent too much time in front of a screen. He wanted help using his time for the things that make him truly happy. He apologized for his attitude and hugged his brothers.

One was feeling great but wanted to be more productive. We thanked him for keeping things happy and light.

And one just wanted hugs after school. A pretty simple request.

As I went to bed that night, I was content and happy instead of agitated and angry. I watched three teenagers and one energetic eight-year-old self reflect, share weaknesses, apologize, forgive, ask for help, and love each other in a group setting. I was amazed and grateful for a husband who took the high road and was a beautiful example of humility and growth.

He wasn't afraid to try something different, to be someone different.

Ten years ago, I never would have imagined that he would be the one to calm things down and parent with love, patience, and understanding while I dealt with my internal struggle to fiercely forge ahead; but I was so proud of how far he had come. **We cannot fault ourselves for slow change; the process was never supposed to be quick and easy,**but look at where it can lead if we let it. His worth, and by association the worth of each family member, was bolstered significantly that day because of his willingness to slowly become someone new.

Where you want to be may seem far from where you are now, but if you invite Christ into your story, anything is possible. Remember the woman with the issue of blood? What if she had become so comfortable on the fringes of society that she hadn't looked for more? What if she wasn't sure if she wanted or deserved a life better than the one she had? What if she stayed stuck in a routine that prevented her healing? What if she believed the lies others told her? Would she have stayed home and missed her chance with Jesus?

Do not miss your chance with Him! Do not settle for a mediocre life, a life of petty jealousy, of underachievement, of status quo, of living below your privileges. You were meant for more.

———————

Exercise #1

In your prayers tonight, ask God what one thing you need to take out of your life, and what one thing you need to add to it. Listen and act.

_____

_____

_____

_____

_____

Exercise #2

Think of who you were 10 years ago. List 10 ways you have significantly improved from the person you used to be. Be sure to focus on the inside changes, not just the obvious ones.

_____

_____

_____

_____

_____

When we take the time to really get to know one another, all that is left between us is love.

CHAPTER 11

Letting Go Of The Ideal Mold

I spent a good portion of my early motherhood years trying to pretend I was someone I wasn't. I wanted to be it all: a list-making mom, a chore-chart mom, a snuggle-before-bed mom, an athletic mom, a science mom, and a musical mom. I especially wanted to be a mom with a sparkling clean home that was full of meticulously-organized drawers. For some reason, in my eyes, those were characteristics great moms would have. When I discovered Pinterest and Instagram, I unconsciously added 20 more ideas of what a perfect mom should look like.

About a year after this motherhood overload started, there was a viral article asking moms to "dial down the holidays." It was real and hilarious and the first of its kind to call out the over-celebrated, overindulgent culture we had so quickly created thanks to social media. I loved it because it justified my lack of creativity and lack of desire to go all out all the time, so I emailed it to all my friends, and they loved it too. Except one. Kim didn't like it much at all.

Kim grew up in a home that didn't have a lot. Money was always tight, and they were forced to make do. They didn't go on vacations; she wasn't enrolled in sports or music lessons; they didn't go to the movies or get summer pool passes; but her mom always celebrated holidays. She could, on her meager income, provide childhood magic with only a couple of extra dollars and a little ingenuity.

They always had themed birthday cakes, leprechaun traps, creative Valentine's boxes, and homemade Halloween costumes long before you could find these ideas on parenting blogs. This was the way her mom showed love and devotion to her children and created happy memories they would rely on during difficult times.

When Kim shared her life experience with me, I didn't know what to say. I was embarrassed because she was right. Why did the way other mothers choose to love their kids matter to me? Why did I feel so much pressure to be everything? Why couldn't I be happy for them and content with myself?

If I was going to make it through motherhood, I would have to find a better perspective, one that allowed each of us to shine and fulfill our own roles in the best possible way. I wanted to honor the worth and talents each woman had been given. As I made a mental shift, the following words came to me:

Holidays could easily make me feel like a mom fail. As I scroll through Facebook and Instagram, it is obvious my little ones are getting the raw end of the deal. My kids are the ones dressed in old sports uniforms for Halloween, and one year I sent them to school with a plastic grocery bag for their Valentine's box. Leprechauns have never visited our home. We tried the Elf on the Shelf, and he only moved once . . . from the tree to the banister.

When notes come home about large, artistic school projects, I groan inside. I am completely incapable of cutting a straight line, which doesn't translate well for science fair boards and large-scale book reports. It's tough to tell the difference between my artistic efforts and those of my kids. I just hate that kind of stuff.

Pinterest has created an even wider chasm between the "haves" and "have nots" when it comes to creativity and patience. It used to be that only the really talented parents could pull off a showstopper; now it's shocking when someone can't.

But, here's the thing. **I LOVE that you can.**

I love going through the Valentine's boxes and seeing darling, homemade cards. I love hearing about the coolest Halloween costumes and seeing really amazing science fair projects. I love that you celebrate the heck out of St. Patrick's Day. I love that my friend makes ridiculously amazing cakes for her kids' birthdays, and that my cousin threw a carnival, complete with cotton candy, clowns, games, and a myriad of other awesome things, when her twins turned one.

I also really love it when you invite us to be a part of all your momentous events.

And, it's not just the mom stuff that I think is incredible. I am in awe of our pediatrician who diagnosed allergies by a line on my son's nose, and women who create their own businesses out of big ideas in cluttered garages, and first-grade teachers completely knock my socks off. Can you imagine throwing a seven-hour birthday party, every day, for 28 six-year-olds and hoping they learn something in the process? I could never do or be any of these things, but I am so glad there are women who can.

We teach our kids that different is good, that life would be boring if everyone were the same. But when people are different than we are, or more pointedly, better than we are at something, it makes us feel insecure—as if them being great all of a sudden makes us less good. That feeling forces us to scramble or insult or dismiss or excuse just to put ourselves back on higher ground.

But instead we sink, and we bring other women down with us.

I don't want people to dial things down so I can feel secure. My friends don't need to hide their talents so I can feel better about myself. I want to live in a community where women can showcase their strengths and pursue their talents at home and in the workforce without the fear of being or looking "too good."

When women excel at anything, it is good for all of us. I love that my kids get to be part of crazy creative class parties and caring playgroups. I'm grateful for intuitive physicians and gentle dentists that keep my boys healthy. And I like bringing what I have to the table too. I like helping with essay writing and reading. I like sharing book lists, favorite museums, and a few good recipes. I like pulling a little extra weight in the classroom or driving to soccer practice while another mom is out on the police force or nursing a newborn.

I spent most of my college years studying literature from a feminist perspective, and in hindsight, I may have had it all wrong. Feminism looks different to me now. To me, a real feminist allows all women to discover what their best self is, and then lets them be that best in a world, nation, and community that refuses to cut down what is painstakingly being built inside the home or outside of it. **We should celebrate the opportunity that women can be anything, from a corporate leader to a killer**

room mom. There is a seat for everyone at the table, and we all benefit when everyone gives their best to make things work.

I had a neighbor who had a talent for making every moment sensational for her family, with visits from the Magic School Bus and themed family home evenings. I had another neighbor who was a concert pianist and so cultured and well-spoken that you wanted to brush up on grammar and philosophy after chatting with her. I had a friend who was consistently generous, funding important causes because of her professional success. Being close to these women didn't make me less successful; I was still me but better, because I learned from their creativity, culture, and goodness.

Many years ago, in a rough moment of motherly inadequacy, I wondered how I could ever measure up to everyone around me. Then, I had a distinct Godly impression, almost a voice that said, "I gave you these boys because they needed YOU to be their mother." It was a beautiful, spiritual experience as I realized who I WAS instead of who I wasn't. My boys didn't need a college professor, a sports star, a party thrower, a decorator, or a perfectly-organized mother; **they just needed me, and I was enough.**

Those words have stayed forefront in my mind for over seven years. Anytime I want to dismiss another mother or criticize her for the way she does things, I remember that I am so glad she can love her kids the way they need to be loved, and I'm so grateful that I can love my kids the way they need to be loved.

This is true in womanhood in general. When we realize we don't have to fit a specific mold, it becomes easy to give others permission to be different and powerful in their own way.

I love Brené Brown's quote that says, "People are hard to hate up close." I have seen that truth manifested to me over and over again. As we open our eyes and our hearts to others, especially to those who are different from us, we begin to understand the worth of a soul much more clearly.

A sweet woman named LeRae received a testimony of this early in her life when she found herself in a very unexpected friendship. Many years ago, she and her husband bought their first house right out of college. It was small with a flat roof and nestled in a rough neighborhood, but it was a loving home to their family of four.

She had a neighbor across the street named Kay. Kay was in her early 30s, had four children from several ex-husbands, and was currently living with Robyn, a 25-year-old rock-and-roll drummer. Needless to say, the two families didn't have much in common.

To make matters worse, one of Kay's teenage sons had recently returned home from juvenile detention, broken into LaRae's home, and slashed the tires on her car. The relationship hadn't gotten off to a great start.

LeRae had been having some health problems and was low on energy and busy with two small kids. So, when a sheet was passed around in Relief Society to sign up to feed Kay's family because of her recent breast cancer diagnosis, LeRae did the "neighborly" thing and signed up to bring something in.

She quickly dropped off the meal on her assigned day, doing her duty but leaving without much thought or concern. She was relieved to be done with the task and didn't think about Kay again, figuring the Relief Society had everything handled. A month or so later, LeRae felt an incessant impression to go and check on Kay. She thought of every excuse to ignore it: she didn't feel well, she didn't know her, they had nothing in common, the ward had it taken care of, and she just couldn't be responsible for everything.

Kay ignored the nudge for a couple of weeks, but the prompting wouldn't leave, so she walked across the street in an effort to regain her peace. When she knocked on the door, it opened slightly, and she said, as quickly as she could, "I am LeRae Archibald, and I live across the street, and if there is ever anything I can do let me know." She turned to walk away when a hand reached out to grab her arm.

She looked back to see Robyn, the tough drummer, with tears streaming down his face. "How did you know we needed help?" Kay's cancer had taken a turn for the worse, she was losing steam, and her young husband had no idea what to do.

So, LaRae stopped her own life and stepped into theirs as she took care of Kay every day. She cleaned Kay's home, helped her bathe, and wrapped her head in a scarf just in time for Robyn to come home.

These two very different women learned to love each other. They lay on the bed together and watched TV and chatted from January until July, when cancer took her feeble friend. At Kay's funeral, there were only 10 in attendance, and LeRae was heartbroken that so many people missed out on knowing and loving Kay the way she did. She learned that **women of worth come dressed in all different outfits, with varied backgrounds, families, and life situations, but when we take the time to really get to know and understand each other, all that is left between us is love**.

It is easy to connect with those who are just like us, who act the way we act and think the way we think, but perhaps there is such variety on this earth for a purpose. Are there lessons to learn, hearts to change, and minds that need to be opened in order to become more like our Savior?

Today, most choose to live their lives in an echo chamber, a place where everyone agrees with them and reinforces their view of the world. When someone doesn't, it is taken as a personal attack with offended parties and people removed from lives and Facebook feeds. This is a dangerous way to live and alienates us from those with whom we could learn and grow. **When we choose not to engage with people who feel and think differently, we miss out on relationships and opportunities to expand our minds and test our own beliefs. We miss out on the joy of diversity.**

Jesus didn't avoid those who were different from Him or only associate in circles that would cheer his every word. No. He discussed important issues with people who were passionately opposed to His way, made many in His presence uncomfortable with his desire for change, and challenged the status quo on a daily basis.

He was peculiar to many but determined to create a better world and society than the one that currently existed. He executed His ideas determinedly and always with an increase of love, even for those who didn't agree. He wasn't afraid to learn from others or dig into the reality of one person's experience and led with hope and action. As always, there is so much we can learn from His example.

I wonder what might have happened if the people of Galilee had made room, somehow, for the woman with the issue of blood? Could their lives have been blessed by the perspective, knowledge, and experience she had to offer? How would her life have changed if someone had brought her in? It wasn't possible or even legal at the time for them to do that, but we don't have the excuses they did. Nothing is stopping us from reaching out, learning, and loving, except ourselves. This is no time to be timid, there is too much to lose. Let's lean in and trade sameness and comfort for the best this world has to offer.

Exercise #1

When has someone completely different from you touched your life? Send them a quick text to let them know how much they mean to you.

_____

_____

_____

_____

_____

Exercise #2

Is there someone in your life who is very different from you? Invite that person into your world. Learn more about his or her family, likes, dislikes and traditions. Be a true friend to them.

_____

_____

_____

_____

_____

The only number that really matters to Jesus is one.

CHAPTER 12

It's Not About The Numbers

We live in a world that is obsessed with numbers and validation, as if what we do is only important if the world says it is or if other people shout our praises from the rooftops. But **when we live for likes, we miss what matters most,** so it is helpful to remember that the only number that really matters to Jesus is one.

There were times when Christ ministered to 5,000, but more often we find Him reaching out to the one. Think of Lazarus, the daughter of Jarius, Mary, Martha, Peter, the woman taken in adultery, and my favorite, the woman with the issue of blood. He didn't save His best moments, His kindest words, His most inspiring miracles for His biggest audiences; He shared them when they were needed most, often just with one.

We must keep in mind that we too are here mostly for just the one. That principle is easy to overlook, especially when we feel excited and inspired about something new. If we are *inspired* to make a job change, start a business or podcast, go back to school, or stay home with our kids, it seems like it should all go smoothly. But sometimes the business never gets off the ground, only our family and close friends listen to our interviews, report cards are full of mediocre grades, and staying home is significantly lonelier than we imagined. It's easy to second guess our spiritual reception and conclude that maybe we were never really inspired at all.

During these times, we must believe in the principle of the one; believe that sometimes the one who needs to be reached or changed is us. **Zoom in, and you will see the effect of your small, faithful decisions.** Your failed business may have started a forever friendship, a podcast interview may be a vital connection for your next great idea, the psychology class you almost failed may have given you clarity on a past relationship, and that year at home gave you unforgettable moments you may need to rely on later.

This quote by Neal A. Maxwell reminds me how crucial each one of us is to our Heavenly Father's plan.

The same God that placed that star in a precise orbit millennia before it appeared over Bethlehem in celebration of the birth of the Babe has given at least equal attention to placement of each of us in precise human orbits so that we may, if we will, illuminate the landscape of our individual lives, so that our light may not only lead others but warm them as well [6]

God is orchestrating a divine purpose and plan through you. You are crucial to what He has in store, so don't stop or give up just because everything doesn't go according to *your* plan.

A wise friend of ours was telling us about all the things he feels inspired to do for his young men at church: the handouts, challenges, texts, temple trips, and other extra opportunities he gives them to grow and feel the Spirit. My husband and I were incredulous, having four boys of our own, and asked if anyone ever takes a challenge or follows up on anything he asks. He said that every now and then one boy will, and it makes all the effort worth it.

As he was talking, I thought about what he said. Because if that ONE boy it made a difference to was MY boy, it would mean everything. I believe that truth is universal. If the one person whose life is changed is the person you love most, wouldn't all the effort be worth it?

When numbers become our measure of fulfillment, there is a good chance we will miss the ONE. And

---

6 *Maxwell, Neal A.That My Family Should Partake. (Salt Lake City: Deseret Book, 1974) 86.*

so, **instead of worrying about the vastness of your influence, about how many people you can reach, how many likes or comments you get, or how many verbal thank-yous you receive, think about how hearing and acting on the Spirit might affect your one, or even someone else's one.** Hearing and following our Savior's voice is ALWAYS worth it.

One Sunday, the reality of this doctrine became very clear to me. Much of my time at church has been spent in the foyer. Something about the sacred quiet always triggered my children's worst behavior, and I often wondered why we even tried to attend when all our time was spent pacing the halls.

I remember envying other parents at church with kids who liked to quietly color and look at books. I fantasized about being an empty nester and wondered what it might be like to just sit and listen on Sunday, bathed in a spiritual halo of inspiration. Instead, I had my reality: Sundays without respite, rejuvenation, or spiritual renewal. Just another week in the foyer.

So on that Sunday, in an effort to get my unruly toddler to calm down, I tried pointing out Jesus in the paintings on the wall. One painting stopped me from moving on. It was Christ with the lost sheep. He left his 99 to go search for the one who had strayed.

It got me thinking that of all the places we might find Jesus in the church, there was a good chance he would be with me, right there in the foyer.

He would be there welcoming the worn-out, single mother and her children who never make it to church on time. He would sit on that stiff, floral sofa next to the woman weeping alone because of heartache. He would shake the hand of the man who decides to walk through the glass doors for the first time in far too long. He would embrace the couple who is too deeply offended to come all the way in, but who miss church desperately. He would smile at the teenager who is strategically avoiding the sacrament, not sure how to take care of the sins that make church so difficult, and He would talk with the woman who has too many doubts to feel like she fits in. He would even walk with me.

For a brief moment, looking at this painting, I was His one. He showed me a glimpse of what my showing up, even when it was hard, meant to my future family. He let me peek into a time when I would miss the Cheerios and crayons strewn all over the bench, and would wish for more one-on-one moments in the church hallway talking about Jesus. He showed me my unruly boys who could never sit still, worshiping quietly and bringing the sacrament to so many in the congregation who desperately need Him.

He taught me to forget about myself for a minute and really see the people in the foyer—those He has been waiting for or worrying about for so long. He asked me to welcome them, to love them, to remind them that He is glad they are here, sins, jeans, questions, tears, and all.

He taught me that day how good it feels to be the one.

Every now and then, someone seems to understand the concept of "the one" so clearly that she ends up changing the world. Lori was this type of woman. She was Sally's (name has been changed) minister. Sally and her family left the Church five years ago because of doctrinal differences. The split was hard spiritually, emotionally, and socially, and they felt rather isolated in their newfound life. They had little contact with the Church, and many of their neighbors were unsure of how to deal with this new situation. But not Lori. Lori was a family favorite. She visited every single month, but more than that, she never missed a chance to care. Her kids were grown, so she loved Sally's children like they were her own. She attended plays, dance recitals, and games. She brought dinner and filled in gaps whenever she was needed.

One month, during her official visit, Sally said, "Lori, you don't have to do this anymore. We are never coming back to the Church, and you are such a good visiting teacher. Someone in your ward deserves to have you, not me."

Lori replied, "Do you think I visit you because I have to or because I am assigned to you? I visit you because I love you. You will never shake me."

October had been busy, and Sally was preparing for a cruise at the end of the month. She and Lori had tried to meet up, but life kept getting in the way, so Sally suggested they just get together when she returned home. But Lori begged, "I have to see you. Please come meet me for lunch before you go."

Sally, also one of the most kind and caring women I know, made time. She brought her little girl and sat with Lori at lunch for over an hour. At the end of the meal, Lori emphasized how much she loved Sally and her family and what a light they were in her life, and Sally was able to vocalize that same love.

A week later, when Sally got off the cruise ship and back on land, her phone lit up with text messages. One particular message stopped her in her tracks. While she had been away, Lori had been hit in an auto-pedestrian accident and they hadn't been able to save her. Sally was devastated, and her family dissolved into tears at the news of losing someone who had shown them so much love.

As Sally told me this story in a choked-up voice, she said, "She was my last connection to our ward. We are going to miss her so much."

How incredible that Lori lived a life where she constantly focused on the one, so that Sally could have the chance to feel of Lori's love and share how much she meant to her family one last time. As I have learned more about Lori after her passing, it has become obvious to me that Sally isn't the only one who saw her as a beacon of Christlike love; everyone who was lucky enough to spend time with her felt the exact same way. She took those who needed her most into her arms and into her heart. What a legacy to leave.

I want to live a life more like Lori's. One where the noise of the world becomes quiet and the voice of the Spirit so familiar, it is impossible to ignore. A life that is focused on the one. I am not there yet, but my desire is to love like she loved and hear like she heard.

I hope you will join me and be better at reaching out, slowing down, quieting our minds, choosing to hear, and living a life full of Christlike love so that one day, someone might say of you and me, "SHE showed me how it felt to be loved. SHE was an answer to my prayer. I couldn't shake her. SHE knew her Savior. One day, I want to be just like her."

Exercise #1

In your morning prayers, ask to be led to one person who needs you, then act on any promptings you receive.

_____

_____

_____

_____

Exercise #2

Make a point to slow down this week and look around. Try to serve the one in small ways every chance you get.

_____

_____

_____

_____

I can find power in the push and joy in the journey.

CHAPTER 13

Ditch
The Perfect

For ten years I struggled with an eating disorder. It took a physical toll on my body, but as I look back, the most heartbreaking part is what it did to my spirit. For so many years, I allowed my worth to be dictated by numbers on a scale, the way a pair of pants fit, or my ability to severely restrict calories. One day, I felt superior to others because of my stellar self-control, and the next day I hated myself because of my weakness.

Perhaps the most disheartening side effect during these years was my constant self-obsession. Most of my thoughts and conversations revolved around food and Exercise because there was no room in my mind or in my life for anything else. The obsession had completely taken over. Looking back, I feel lucky that I had friends and family who saw past the disorder and loved me anyway.

As I started to heal and to let go of old ideals and beliefs, for the first time in many years, my mind was free. I was free to be more than a body, and I could talk about more than health and fitness. I was interesting and interested again. I had the time and energy to be a friend, to think deeply, to create. There was space in my heart to receive revelation and understand my own divine worth, completely independent from my scale. I started to love myself again and discover more of who I was meant to be. I let go of that ideal woman and started being happy with the woman I already was.

Because of this experience and the deep happiness I found through healing, I tend to revolt against anything that comes close to requiring perfection.

One day, I was sitting in an audience during a gathering of women when the speakers started talking about President Nelson's 5 pillars to unlock the power of heaven. Part of the quote they shared had to do with EXACT obedience, and I cringed. This phrase has always been a hard one for me because since those calorie-counting days, I have never been exact at anything. I don't close drawers, I enter events into my Google calendar at "approximate" times, and I believe "ballpark" and "good enough" will make do in nearly every situation. I am not a list maker; I can't be trusted with cash; and I still lose my shoes from time to time. Now you see why exact obedience is tough for me. Chances are, heaven will be out of reach if exact anything is a qualification. As the speakers continued, I started to doodle in my notebook and squirm in my seat, trying to determine if meeting four out of five of President Nelson's pillars would be good enough for at least a peek into heaven.

I anxiously continued partially listening, but my ears perked up as the discussion deepened as to what "exact obedience" truly meant. Emily Belle Freeman, a spiritual hero of mine, gave two examples of exact obedience from the scriptures: Jesus and the Pharisees. Both were exactly obedient, one to the Spirit and inspiration, and the other to the letter of the law.

After further explanation, exact obedience finally made sense and seemed like a possibility, even for a rather chaotic soul like myself. I could live a life that was close to the Spirit and act on inspiration much more easily than I could check off a list of lofty ideals. For the first time, I realized that **exact obedience has nothing to do with our earthly idea of perfection and everything to do with being perfected in Christ.** It was freeing and empowering. All of a sudden, opening the heavens didn't seem so impossible, even for me.

As a young mom, I remember desperately wanting to have heavenly family home evenings. I wanted them to be spiritual, full of love, creative, fun, and exciting. I would prepare and follow ideas I had seen in packets or heard about through Relief Society activities. I spent a good amount of time on preparation, but nothing ever went as well as I hoped it would. My three young boys did not buy into the celestial vision I had been trying to make happen, and quite honestly they seemed intent on actively working against it.

One Tuesday morning, after an especially disappointing Monday evening, I was frustrated and annoyed and knew something had to change. I let go of that "ideal" family I so badly wanted us to be, and started working with who we really were. Family home evenings changed. A song, a prayer, a QUICK lesson from the *Friend*, chocolate chips for dessert, and lots of wrestling and outdoor playing to end the night. A lot less fluff, work, and annoyance, and a whole lot more family and home in our evening.

No one would have recorded our activities for a Mormon Ad or written about our creative methods on a gospel blog, but we were doing the important things: teaching the gospel and loving each other. I wasn't sure why I had spent so much time overcomplicating it all in the first place. We found satisfaction in this type of exact obedience and knowing our hearts were in the right place.

In a world full of filtered images, highly competitive achievers, and mirages of perfection, our kids are desperate for these same reminders. Parental pressure, outside influences, and inward grit push children of all ages to think the ideal is the only option, and they are crumbling because of it.

It's easy to unconsciously feed into this standard if you have a competitive child who obeys and aims to please, because who doesn't enjoy seeing their kid rack up all the gold stars? This is why it is critical to remind our children often that neither our love nor God's love is based on star performances or mistake-free living. One of my sons leans toward this impossible ideal. One night I pulled him aside and said:

> You are an amazing kid, but we know you are not perfect. You have made mistakes, and you will continue to make more because you are mortal. You will do things you are not proud of. You will see something inappropriate and like it. You will fail a test or forget to turn something in. You will say words you know you shouldn't, laugh at a mean joke, and be a jerk when you should be kind. We already know this will happen, and we love you anyway.
>
> Please tell us when you are struggling and need help. We will still think you are phenomenal. The worst thing you can do is keep hard things hidden. They will eat you up inside. Open up and admit when you are wrong. Tell us when you are weak

and how we can help. There will be consequences, but you can get through them, and you will come out on the other side so much better and so much stronger. Please know that you can always be forgiven, by us and by God; you have a million chances to make things right, and you can work through anything. We are always here for you. So while we appreciate your awesomeness, we would never expect you to be perfect.

This took a weight off his shoulders and started a conversation that needed to happen. We all need to believe those words, about our children but also about ourselves.

As a newlywed, I was sitting in a sacrament meeting when a young husband shared an experience I will never forget. His talk was on the Atonement, and he said that one Sunday, when he didn't take the sacrament, his mom put her arm around him and whispered, "I am so proud of you for taking the Atonement seriously. If you ever need me, you know I am here for you." From that moment, I knew I wanted to be that kind of mom.

Letting go of unrealistic expectations for ourselves and our children brings about a healthy openness and allows everyone the freedom to become something more. This closeness, this acceptance, and this connection just might remind you that reality is even better than ideal.

I've noticed that even with an open heart and feet planted in reality, life has a way of derailing us. There are times when we freeze, unwilling and often unable to take even a tiny step or force an inch of progress because of life circumstances. In the fall of 2019, I went through a time like this. My dad, the healthiest and smartest 63-year-old out there, had a rare virus attack his brain, putting him in a coma in the neu-ro-ICU unit for months. At the same time, we were dealing with exceptionally difficult kid problems that brought heartache and forced hard change. To top it off, my husband had just started a challenging job with a hefty commute. Pile on hours at the hospital, uncertainty in every area of life, and all the regular ups and downs every family encounters, and it was all just too much. I felt intense heaviness all the time.

One Saturday, in an effort to escape the pounding of daily life, we headed to the mountains, where we completed one lovely hike. But it was quick and we had time for more, so we ventured out on hike number two. Within a few minutes it was obvious that we were in for more than we bargained for. It was hot and steep, and every step burned.

My kids were complaining, and I was feeling men-tally and physically weak. We were halfway through when my youngest stopped and declared through screaming and tears that he would not continue. I offered to stay with him. Honestly, he was just voicing the way I felt too, and I wanted an excuse to quit without looking wimpy to my especially-fit husband.

But then, my 12-year-old, who also wasn't happy about the never-ending incline, turned to him and said, "You know they aren't going to let you stop, so you might as well keep going." He was right, about the hike and about life. We would just have to keep going.

We paused to regroup, and my husband put our way-too-heavy eight-year-old on his back for a little break. As we continued up the trail, we passed a group of happy hikers and realized that this experience could either be miserable and painful, or full of improvement and purpose. It would be up to us.

That hiking lesson hit me hard because it was exactly what needed to be done in my daily life. I needed to change my focus. I needed to look up and look out. I needed to see the good and recognize the hand of God. I needed to be grateful for growth and the blessing of walking a difficult road buoyed up by those I love. Yes, there would be times I needed to stop and rest or even have someone carry me during the hardest parts, but that's okay. A loving God had woven those options into the plan because He knew life wouldn't be perfect.

I would keep reminding myself about the necessity of hard things, that no one gets to walk downhill all the time, and of the invaluable perspective from the top of what looks like an insurmountable obstacle. **I would continue. I would bring back the smile and find "power in the push" and joy in the journey.**

If your heart is too heavy for you to bear, your head is barely above water, and nothing is like you hoped it would be, I send you all my love. This isn't easy, but the world needs your light, so keep going. Look up. Reach out. Hold on. He's got you.

That September Saturday wasn't the first time I had felt that sort of desperate need for relief and perspective. A few years ago, I was in a yoga class, and as we were winding down and practicing stillness, the instructor told us to try some self-affirmation. She suggested starting with the words "I AM," and filling in the blanks. She gave us some ideas: Amazing. Beautiful. Enough. But those words didn't work for me. My life was a mess. I was falling short of every expectation I had for myself and I felt like I was disappointing God. I grasped for a word that would honestly finish that "I AM" sentence, but only one word would come: TRYING.

It didn't seem very affirming, and that morning, in the stillness, my inadequacies felt larger than life.

I was questioning my parenting, my priorities, my writing, my nutrition, the way I used my time, my spiritual discipline, if I was reaching out enough, if I showed enough love to my spouse—the list seemed miles long.

However, one thing was confirmed to me in that dark, quiet moment: I was TRYING. I was trying to be better. I was trying to love and learn and grow and forgive. I was trying to see people the way God sees them, and I needed to see myself with those same generous eyes.

I knew I had a lot of work to do, but boy was I trying. If I am being honest, I felt a little sorry for myself walking out of the fitness room that day. I imagined what the other women's powerful words might have been while mine was just "trying." I wanted something more celebratory or bold, then God told me how He felt about trying:

Trying is beautiful, successful, amazing, bold, and enough. Trying is everything.

———

Exercise #1

Make a list of the areas in your life where you are truly trying, but the outcome is not what you hoped it would be. How have you grown and changed in good ways through the process?

_____

_____

_____

_____

Exercise #2

Who, in your life, needs to understand that progress is more important than perfection? Discuss these ideas with him or her and help them understand how unconditional your love and God's love is.

_____

_____

_____

_____

I am
okay with
imperfections
in others
because I
recognize how
often others are
okay with the
imperfections
in me.

CHAPTER 14

Give Them Some Grace

A few years ago, our family decided to read scriptures early in the morning before our kids headed out for school. This was not an ideal time for one son; he hated mornings and wasn't particularly fond of the scriptures. We invited him to join us, but most days he would roll out of bed with just enough time to make it to school before the bell rang.

Every once in a while, and mostly on accident, he would appear for family scripture study. Those mornings were lighter and happier, and we were so proud of him and grateful for his efforts. One day, he came to me and said, "It seems like you guys only like me on days I show up for scriptures."

His honesty hit me hard because there was a little truth to it. In an effort to encourage good behavior, we had been especially pleased and loving on the days he had joined us for scripture study, and apparently (but unknowingly) harsh and dismissive on the days he missed. This was unacceptable and absolutely contrary to the way Christ taught His gospel. He invited all to come unto Him, and when people chose not to, He loved them anyway. He was comfortable living a gospel-centered life and shared it with others, but showed His love equally to those who believed and those who did not. We needed to internalize Christ's words and example more fully in our home.

I talked with my husband and things changed immediately. We wanted our son there with us and we consistently invited him, but we made sure he knew that our love for him had nothing to do with his daily spiritual habits. As he felt that love, he opened up and confided in us. He shared problems, fears, and worries. He began to engage in spiritual moments in small ways, and a few (long) years later was engaged in the gospel again through a series of small miracles that we will never take for granted. **Agency and love did not push him away. They kept him anchored to us during the times he needed us most.**

It can be so easy for us to expect the impossible from others and live our life in constant disappointment. I am certain that was never part of God's plan. I love the quote from Elder Renlund in 2015 that says,

"Just as God rejoices when we persevere, He is disappointed if we do not recognize that others are trying too. . . . As God encourages us to keep on trying, He expects us to also allow others the space to do the same, at their own pace."[7]

This quote pierced me. It can be so easy to assume we all have the same strengths, feelings, testimonies, and abilities, and that what comes easily to me, comes easily to you. These kinds of assumptions lead to unrealistic expectations, hurt feelings, and sometimes, ruined relationships. Can we give those we love, and even those we don't, a little more space on their path? Can we let them progress at their own pace? The gift of grace goes such a long way.

In *The Seven Principles for Making Marriage Work*, Dr. John Gottman's research shows that 69% of problems in a relationship are perpetually unsolvable. When I read that statistic, I was floored and quite disappointed, until I realized how much freedom that number gave me. I could quit trying to change my partner or others that I care about, and work on seeing the good and loving them instead. A huge weight had been lifted, and my perspective shifted significantly.

Instead of my husband "lacking contentment," I could see him as adventurous. I could appreciate his desire for new places, people, and experiences

---

7   *Dale G. Renlund, "Latter Day Saints Keep On Trying," Ensign, May 2015: https://www.churchofjesuschrist.org/study/general-conference/2015/04/latter-day-saints-keep-on-trying?lang=eng*

instead of feeling threatened by it. And I could be grateful for all that he had introduced our family to because of this exceptional, not annoying, quality. In contrast, he could start seeing my contentment as a gift instead of "boring," and appreciate my easygoing nature and easily-pleased attitude. One quality was not better than the other; they were just different and both contributed to a happy home. This new way of looking at each other has been so helpful as we try to play off one another's strengths and willingly make up for weak spots too.

This type of grace extends well beyond marriages. It looks like enjoying and learning from the way your in-laws do things, even if it is completely opposite from the way you grew up. It looks like holding your tongue when someone executes an idea in a way you would never choose. It looks like trying to understand a person's background, talents, and weaknesses, and filling in where they lack instead of whispering about their failures. It looks like finding solutions together instead of complaining about the outcome. And it looks like a lot of self-reflection, and being grateful for all the times others held their tongues, made up for your lack, or filled in your gaps. **It is being okay with the imperfection of others because you recognize how often others are okay with the imperfection in you.**

My friend Laurrie offered so much grace to me when

I was nothing but a disappointment.

One Sunday at church, I saw her wrestling her two grandbabies during sacrament meeting. This young and fit new grandma looked tired and overwhelmed with all of their energy. I caught up with her after the meeting and asked if she was babysitting. She replied that her daughter and son-in-law had gone on vacation for 11 days, and she was in charge. I asked how many days they had already been gone, and she replied, "Two." She said it had already been tough, and she was exhausted. She had forgotten how hard it was to be a young mom and wondered how she had ever done it! I resolved to help her that week, by taking the girls for a bit to give her a little break.

I felt the impression on Monday that she needed me. But I really don't like to babysit, so I decided I would wait until Thursday, when she was desperate—then my service would really make a difference. The next day, I had the same impression, but I still really didn't want to babysit. I rationalized again and decided that I would bring her a meal or something else instead. You know, outsmart the Spirit and check the box. Well, the week got busy, and I never helped babysit. I didn't bring a meal. I didn't even drop by to keep her company.

Two Sundays later, during a combined meeting, we were asked to share how someone had listened to the

Spirit and met our needs.

Laurrie, with tears in her eyes and a shaky voice, shared how difficult her week had been without one moment to herself. She was short on sleep and time, and just exhausted in every way, so she prayed for relief. Soon after, Julie came to the rescue to give her a little time to refresh and regroup. Julie was an answer to Laurrie's prayer and reminded her that Heavenly Father really does listen and care.

As I heard Laurrie share her gratitude, I thought, "That should have been you. YOU could have been an answer to her prayers. YOU could have alleviated her sadness and discomfort. YOU could have built your relationship with your friend." I was devastated that I had missed an opportunity to be there for someone who needed me.

I decided to tell Laurrie that I, too, had felt like she needed me that week, but I had ignored the prompting, and I was sorry that I had missed a chance to love and serve her. She was kind, forgiving, and loving in return. She was grateful to know that Heavenly Father really was looking out for her in multiple ways.

I had no excuse but selfishness, and Laurrie still gave me all the grace. It was a beautiful gift because I was already plenty hard on myself for choosing not to be an answer to a prayer. This instance taught me another eternal truth: **Heavenly Father will take care of His children, and He will move His work along with or without us. We are the ones who miss out when we choose not to hear Him.** He had plans for me, He needed me, He trusted me, and I missed out. I never wanted to let my Savior or my friends down like that again.

But I know I will. My selfishness will get in the way again, or busyness will cloud my day, so thank goodness for people who still choose to see my goodness and for a God who does the same. The least I can do in return is to have that same generous spirit with my children, husband, friends, and strangers. I can cheer for them along their path, lift them up when they fall, and embrace their imperfections in a way that lets them know that they are loved, wanted, and needed just the way they are.

———

Exercise #1

Review your expectations for those in your immediate family. Are they realistic? Decide who needs more grace and how you will give it to them.

_____

_____

_____

_____

_____

Exercise #2

Thank someone personally who has overlooked your faults and weaknesses. Let them know how much it means to you to be loved unconditionally.

_____

_____

_____

_____

_____

We must stop glorifying multi-tasking and start praising true, undistracted presence.

CHAPTER 15

Be Still

One key to worth for the woman with the issue of blood was most likely the many hours she sat in stillness. She was forced to be removed from mainstream society which likely gave her time to be alone with her own thoughts, time to be immersed in the scriptures, and time to communicate with God. I am guessing she got really good at listening as the Spirit testified and told her what was true, what to question, and when to act. Her stillness likely brought about true sanctification.

I, on the other hand, like living life on the go. In fact, before being constantly plugged in was a thing, I was already rebelling against stillness. I was the girl who read a book while showering and blow-drying her hair. My bedroom radio was always on, and every time there was a free phone line, I was putting it to good use. I was thrilled with the advent of the smartphone, which brought with it 24/7 access to knowledge, entertainment, and connection. I was feeding myself a constant barrage of information, and I was taking it in as quickly as my mind would allow.

Much of it was good. There was inspiration and

knowledge from podcasts and news articles, opportunities to increase talents and connect with friends, and chances to learn best practices for just about anything and everything without paying a dime.

For a while, I thrived in this environment, but slowly I felt it sucking away my spirit. Instead of gaining knowledge, I was just consuming it and never feeling satisfied. Instead of adding connection, I was adding insecurity and a renewed need to be liked. Instead of enlightenment, I was adding confusion. I realized **too much of a good thing is still too much**. I had filled every second of every day with noise and input, leaving no room in my life to stop, listen, or feel.

When I realized what was happening, I knew something needed to change. I needed to slow down my frenetic pace and leave time for God. I needed connection with the Almighty, through the Spirit, because if I wanted to embrace my imperfections, the imperfections of others, and still find peace and joy, I needed peace and stillness.

Right around this time, I started practicing yoga and I was incredibly uncomfortable with the five minutes of quiet they give you at the end of every class. I had no idea what to do or what to think about when left alone with my own thoughts, but this class allowed me to practice. As I became more comfortable with it, I began to add moments of silence throughout my day, consciously choosing stillness. It would often be in the car, shower, or while cleaning. As I began to add stillness to my life, I started to receive inspiration, and not just for what I needed to "do," but in regards to who I already am. In that stillness, I received ideas and promptings pertaining to my role as a wife, mother, and friend. I started to notice what I needed to change in my life and the messages I needed to share. This inspiration was invigorating, and I began to crave more moments of stillness and looked forward to any chance I had to pause and rest in the quiet.

I also took time to purposely be in nature. Nature made God feel close and allowed me to feel big, important, and alive for all the right reasons. The places without cell service were best because they forced me to focus on the present and feel enduring gratitude for the gift of life.

I made conscious, deliberate choices to put my phone away and be present. This gave me a chance to watch—truly watch—my kids play, and when I did, I was flooded with gratitude. I marveled at their healthy bodies, what great friends they were, and how lucky I was to be in their lives. Anytime I did this, it was impossible not to see the good.

When distractions are gone, there is time to just be.

If you take advantage of that quiet, that stillness, you will be surprised at what you discover: crisp air, happy laughter, warm sunshine, a home, healthy food, a body that moves, a mind that thinks, a heart that can touch another. Worth.

I wonder if God is consistently trying to remind us of how much we mean to Him, of our divine potential and the goodness of others, but we just don't have the time, patience, or space to listen. Surely Satan rejoices when he gets a good woman to dedicate herself to things that don't matter, to habits that slowly, subtly whittle away her self-confidence, drive, and desire. How much of your life is consumed by something that fits into that category?

Our families and friends are starving for our attention. They want to know they matter to us, that what is real is more important than what is fabricated. Could God be feeling the same way? **What great, eternal truths might we be trading for mind-numbing busyness?**

We have to stop glorifying multi-tasking and start praising true, undistracted presence—giving our whole heart and all of our attention to a person, a thought, an experience, or even to stillness itself. What might we discover if we allow ourselves to just be?

For the last 20 years, my dad has used swimming as his form of Exercise. He is in the water for 90 minutes every morning, swimming lap after lap. I cannot think of anything more boring, and his love for music is unprecedented, so I thought waterproof earbuds would be the perfect gift. When I asked my dad if he was interested, he said, "Oh no. That is my time to talk to my Heavenly Father. We converse every morning, and I love it. I go through each member of my family and pray for each of you individually, and then I just talk to Him and let Him talk to me. I would never trade that time with Him for anything." My dad loves his silent morning swims with God.

This year hasn't gone as planned for him with a serious illness, brain injury, and time in a coma. His recovery has not been quick, easy, or complete, but his trust in God and his love and appreciation for those he has prayed for and who have prayed for him, has never wavered. He has spent his life building a relationship with his Father in Heaven, who continues to sustain him. He has never questioned God or asked why. My dad accepts, learns, and loves with a smile, sharing his story and faith with everyone he meets. His willingness to vocally thank God for every little thing, every memory, every person is inspiring and worth emulating. We could all use more morning swims with God.

I want to know God like my dad does, and that

means finding time for stillness. I have so far to go, but I am working hard to make small changes. I am beginning to understand what it means to have a constant prayer in my heart and how to let my Heavenly Father know that I am open to His gentle tutoring each day. I hope He has started to trust me and knows there is room for Him in my life.

I never understood how much I was missing when I was constantly plugged in. During that time, I was getting my worth from the world, and surprisingly enough, most of what was offered there felt rather hollow. When I was willing to be still, even for just a couple of minutes, I began to get glimpses of who I am to God, and that was so much more valuable than anything else I found in the apps and articles I was constantly consuming.

Challenge yourself to be still. Take time to pray, to study, to read, to meditate, and to let yourself FEEL the glorious feeling of being seen, heard, and loved by God.

Exercise #1

Schedule quiet time in your life when you can just stop and listen. No TV, no radio, no podcast, no phone, just silence. Start with five minutes and work your way up.

_____

_____

_____

_____

Exercise #2

Get outside for a minimum of 10 minutes each day without being tethered to any technology. Notice the world around you. Breathe. See if this changes your mood and heart.

_____

_____

_____

_____

Apologizing regularly builds relationships, normalizes mistakes, models remorse, and demonstrates forgiveness with an increase of love.

_____

CHAPTER 16

Do I Really Have To Forgive?

Forgiveness has always been fairly simple in my mind. I have found it easy to give others the benefit of the doubt and assume the best. Then, I had kids, and my inner mama bear came out fiercely.

Kids' feelings are hurt often. It's a challenge, as a parent, to watch this happen and shake it off, but with a little practice it's doable. Then one particular incident tested me to my limit. The cruelty toward my child seemed so significant, it became my obsession. I wanted the kids who had hurt my son to pay, to suffer, to be sorry for what they had done. But I knew that interfering would just make things worse, so on the outside, I had to let it be. Instead, it ate me up inside.

This angry, vengeful way of thinking blocked my normal access to the Spirit and changed who I was. My usually happy, supportive demeanor was harsh and angry. I had no energy to improve myself or dive into spiritual things; there was no space in my heart for good. Instead I stewed, I moped, I gossiped.

One day I realized I no longer liked who I had become. I used to be so full of love and joy, but suddenly I could feel neither. I didn't have time for anyone, my mind was too full, and I even started to wonder if being a good person was worth it if pain and unfairness followed anyway. My days felt dark, and I became guarded and angry.

A few weeks later, I realized that my son, the one who had actually been wronged, the one I was righteously indignant for, had made peace and moved on. The kids I was so angry with didn't even know or care, but I was suffering as I harbored the unsettled feelings of resentment. I wasn't ready to let the hurt go, but it was time. Something had to change.

Unfortunately, the feelings didn't leave quickly or with one repentant prayer; however, they did lessen. I pleaded for a change of heart. It wasn't about repenting for being wrong, or mean, or bad, but it was asking Christ to come into my heart and change my desires, my understanding. I needed Him to allow me to see the people who had wronged us in a new light. I wanted Him to open my eyes to an alternative perspective. When I asked with real intent, healing slowly started to happen. My desire for revenge and vilification decreased. I found myself going an entire day without thinking about how hurt I was. Then I went two days. When someone asked about the situation, I chose to say, "It's good" instead of digging into details. I started to enjoy life and have conversations that didn't revolve around my hurt. Slowly, I started to feel like myself again; I found joy and even began to understand the truth of Romans 8:28, which says, **"And we know that all things work together for good to them that love God. . ."**

After I let things go and was on a path of forgiveness, I was able to see that what had previously felt so cruel and unfair was surprisingly working for our good. The unkind actions of a few had pushed us in a new direction, one that was significantly better, more peaceful, and full of opportunity. All the bad had led to a miracle that we had been pleading for for three years. God certainly works in mysterious ways.

As I acknowledged this, my heart softened and I could be grateful for the way Heavenly Father watched out for us: allowing us to go through really dark, difficult things in order to bring about something better than we could have imagined. We don't "deserve" hard things; sometimes they just come. But when they happen, we can choose to embrace our new circumstance and grow and change, or we can stay stuck, inhibiting our own happiness and progress.

If there is one Christlike quality we can use more than anything else as mothers, I be-

lieve it is forgiveness— forgiveness of others and of ourselves. There is nothing like watching your child hurt or suffer at the hands of others, or even by their own doing, to make that mama bear roar inside until all logic and perspective are gone. The pain seems to hurt us twice as much because we feel theirs, and then feel our own.

What we so easily forget is how often our own children, or even we as parents, will naturally be on the giving end of that same hurt or exclusion. Sometimes it is because of circumstance, carelessness, or accident, and other times because of cruelty, anger, or hate. It's embarrassing, sad, and wrong, but it happens.

I sat next to a mom one day who couldn't say enough good things about her daughter: so kind, responsible, smart, talented, trustworthy, and an absolute joy. The very next day, another mom complained to me about the same girl, emphasizing how hard, exclusive, and mean she had been all year and what trouble she had caused.

We all see the world through our own children's lens, which is often filtered to cast them in the most flattering light, but we rarely know the whole truth, and even when we do, people make mistakes. I've watched the best kid I know completely shun someone who desperately needed a friend. I've heard good teenagers use words that floored me and have been shocked by the disrespect and ingratitude shown by really GREAT kids from really stellar homes. Why? Because they are children, and we have to remember that.

I've seen parents rocked by the unfairness of the system for one child, then turn around and take advantage of it when it worked in the favor of another. I've seen moms cry and complain when their child was ostracized, but when things were going well for child number two, they didn't worry much about the neighbor who was never included. Why does this happen? **Because we are all imperfect, because parenting is hard, and because we are all still learning**.

This need for forgiveness doesn't stop with the outside world, but is perhaps most important in our own homes. As parents, we will absolutely do things wrong, sometimes in a big way, and **apologizing often can build relationships, show that it is okay to make mistakes, model how to be sincerely sorry, and demonstrate how to forgive with an increase of love.**

In the beginning, I didn't think I could show weakness as a parent, but when I allowed softness and humility to come into our home, things changed. When I started admitting when I was wrong, overreacting, or jumping to conclusions, my kids forgave so easily and became comfortable apologizing for their own mistakes. We created a home of people that didn't love each other because of perfect behavior but in spite of it, and that has allowed our home to be a laboratory where we all learn how to have healthy, honest, relationships with imperfect people.

This new direction also allowed us as parents to forgive ourselves more willingly and often, which has been such a gift in our lives as we navigate difficult situations. Hopefully these lessons will extend beyond the walls of our home.

I know that forgiveness isn't always that simple, that sometimes the hurt and pain take years of therapy and healing to repair, and that we often have to forgive people who don't apologize and are not sorry. I realize certain relationships are more complicated and harmful and need to be worked through carefully. I know specific people need to be kept at a safe distance. I also know that God is on our side, and that the sweet morning of forgiveness is worth the bitter steps it takes to get there.

God has taken care of me and my family, and I am certain that things really can work for our good, eventually, if we will turn to Him. I am grateful to a Savior who made this possible. Only He can make what was wrong, right and what was unfair, fair.

Only because of Him can we let go of our pride and acknowledge our own imperfections. We must be willing to turn to Him in our most agonizing times and let Him take the pain He has already paid for. This willingness allows us to forgive others as He has forgiven us. These actions will prepare us to approach our Savior with confidence, knowing we have given others the same grace He has given to us, over and over again.

———

Exercise #1

Is there someone you need to forgive right now in order to feel in harmony with God? Pray for feelings of forgiveness and understanding to come over you.

_____

_____

_____

_____

Exercise #2

Who do you need to ask forgiveness from? Gather your courage and apologize to someone you may have hurt.

_____

_____

_____

_____

God loves variety.

CHAPTER 17

We All Have A Story

If anyone had a different story than "picture perfect," it was the woman with the issue of blood. She grew up having the Proverb of the Virtuous Woman recited to her daily. She was supposed to be married. She was supposed to have children. Instead, she was alone, an outcast, an embarrassment. Surely the gap between where she was and where she thought she would be was wider than she could have ever imagined.

This same gap exists in all of our lives for a million different reasons, sometimes by choice and other times by chance. When we fixate on who we wish we were or what we wish our life looked like, our insecurity causes us to feel unsure, guarded sometimes even a bit guilty for no real reason at all. It's no surprise that this woman had similar feelings as she approached Christ.

Mark 5:33: "But the woman fearing and trembling, knowing what was done in her, came and fell down before him, and told him all the truth."

She was scared and worried, but she told Jesus "all the truth" about who she was and what she needed from Him. She risked it all because she understood He was her only chance at real change. Though she was physically unworthy she knew something true within herself. She knew that He was ready and waiting for her.

Sometimes we forget His power. Sometimes we think our story is too different to find a place with Him or with others who seem to fit in so easily. This is a falsehood told to us by the great deceiver. He makes us think that if we are not ideal, we have no business being part of anything. This is why, especially during those times, we must continue to show up, to work, to find purpose in unexpected circumstances, and to embrace "all the truth."

It has been amazing to watch good friends find peace and satisfaction in so many different life circumstances. One wraps herself in motherhood, traveling, homeschooling, and creating; another chooses to work full time and finds great child care while another is forced to work and is balancing as best she can. Some struggle with chronic illness and find ways to touch others' lives from bed or in short bursts of daily energy, while others are single and accomplishing great personal and professional goals. Some find joy inside the home while others feel called to be forces in their community, and some need structure and downtime while others thrive on spontaneous engagement.

There is great solace in the words of Elder M. Russell Ballard's BYU Women's Conference address from 2015:

Each of you must come to know what the Lord wants for you individually, given the choices before you. . . .

Once you know the Lord's will, you can then move forward in faith to fulfill your individual purpose. One sister may be inspired to continue her education and attend medical school, allowing her to have a significant impact on her patients and to advance medical research. For another sister, inspiration may lead her to forego a scholarship to a prestigious institution and instead begin a family much earlier than has become common in this generation, allowing her to make a significant and eternal impact on her children now.

Is it possible for two similarly faithful women to receive such different responses to the same basic questions?

Absolutely! What's right for one woman may not be right for another. That's why it is so important that we should not question each other's choices or the inspiration behind them. [8]

Isn't it comforting to know that God has a personal plan for each of us and that we don't have to worry or question the path another woman chooses to take? Many of us are good about embracing variation in others' lives, but can seriously struggle to give ourselves grace when *our* life doesn't go according to plan.

In September, I was invited to a women's retreat that was full of goodness and spiritual light. The culmination of the two days was to attend a session in the Salt Lake Temple with our own family names. Life had been busy and stressful with my dad in the hospital and struggles at home. Add onto that my inexperience with family history and a general feeling of complete overwhelm, and I ended up at the event without a family name.

Because I was unprepared, I considered leaving before the temple session to avoid embarrassment, but I decided it was more important for me to attend unprepared than to not attend at all. Seventy of us walked into the temple together and stood in line to hand over our well-researched names. The woman

---

8 Ballard, M. Russel. *"Women of Dedication, Faith, Determination, and Action."* 1 May 2015. BYU Women's Conference. Transcript. *https://womensconference.ce.byu.edu/sites/womensconference.ce.byu. edu/files/elder_m_russell_ballard_0.pdf*

who usually provides a name to those who come without their own was shocked and so impressed that each person was doing work for someone from their own family. She kept whisper-exclaiming what wonderful women we were. Waiting in line, I felt smaller and smaller, sad that I had shirked such a simple duty. I thought one more time about turning around, but I stayed in line, rehearsing my slacker excuse as I inched closer to her.

When it was my turn, I smiled and quietly told her that I didn't bring my own name, hoping no one in the line of women was looking or listening. But the woman behind me said, "Wait. You don't have your own name? Would you mind doing this one? I brought two, and I would love to have them done together."

I was happy to help and went through the temple for her ancestor instead of mine. Later, I got this message:

Dear Brooke,
You were such an answer to prayer yesterday in the temple and a reminder that God really is watching over each of us and the desires of our hearts. When I was doing the initia-tories for those two names earlier this month I realized they were sisters and had the impression that they should receive their endowments in the same session. At the temple, I was a little sad as it seemed everyone had brought a name and

had resigned myself to just doing one. I didn't want to create a ruckus trying to find someone to do the other name. But there you were, right in front of me. You were there for my second name. A reminder from heaven that God knows our hearts and desires and does amazing things to orchestrate goodness in our lives. Thank you for being there and being available. I have a vision of those two sisters progressing together. What a glorious work we are part of. Thank you for being a woman of light in my life.

Earlier that day, I thought about leaving, about turning around because I wasn't living up to the ideal that I saw in front of me. I certainly didn't feel like a woman of light, but I learned that God needed me and would use me in my imperfect state to accomplish His work. He understood my willing heart in addition to my lack of time and energy, and He consecrated my actions to glorify His purpose. What if I had walked away?

I meet so many women who feel that because they don't fit the mold of what a disciple looks like, talks like, thinks like, sounds like, and acts like, that there is no room for them in this gospel, but that just isn't true. While your opinions and ways of thinking may be different, they are oh so needed! This gospel is a living, breathing organization with growth and change happening regularly. Don't walk away and miss out on the pivotal role you will play for others and in the grand plan of goodness, just because someone might dismiss your way of doing or thinking as "going against the grain." And do not dismiss yourself. Recognize the worth you personally have in moving God's work along.

One Sunday, after voicing some of my wrestles with certain doctrines we were studying, a friend who has spent many years in his own wrestle stopped me and said something to this effect, "You know, not everything always makes sense, and sometimes I don't even know if it's all right, but I know I believe in Jesus and the Atonement, and this gospel is the best way for me to get to Him. When I see it as a vehicle to help me know my Savior, access God and live a life that feels in harmony with them, I don't need the gospel or the people in it to be perfect or infallible. I appreciate it for helping me find Him."

One of my favorite pieces of advice recently was to be gentle with ourselves and each other when it comes to religion. Some feel change is happening too fast while others feel it is not fast enough. Some love the traditions of the past while others are excited about the future. Give each person the room, space, and love they need to progress on their own spiritual path and still feel like part of the fold.

You might never know of the men and women who are holding onto your light, who see themselves in

you, and who have been patiently waiting for someone they identify with. You don't hear their sigh of
relief when you speak, or see the sparkle in their eye
when you share a testimony-building experience. You
have no idea that you might be their reason to stay.
Please remember that God loves variety.

If you are trying desperately to come back to God
but are sure you don't fit in, we need you too. He
needs you. Some say you must decide which side you
are on, that you can't keep sitting on the fence, but
they are wrong. We will take half of you. We will
take you on that fence. We will take you with your
sins and questions, with your quirky habits and out-
landish ideas, because Jesus likes us all and this is His
church. We will wait with you and love you as you
are. That is the gospel, and if others act differently,
please have patience with their frailties too. We are
all still learning.

When that imperfect, ostracized woman approached
Christ, she came to Him from behind (Matt 9:20).
Perhaps she felt that wash of shame so many of us
feel when we come face to face with our own shortcomings. It can be hard to believe we are worth His
goodness. But she pushed through those condemning
thoughts, and reached for the Savior anyway, and
was healed.

After experiencing such a miracle, one would expect

the woman to be fully changed, to radiate confidence, but she still tried to hide (Luke 8:47). Like so many of us might do, she let herself be caught in old patterns and limiting beliefs.

At first, she doesn't believe she deserves what has been offered to her. Then, she allows herself to accept His gift and internalize His healing. When she deeply believes what she already knows, she is fully transformed. She realizes that Jesus knows HER, He feels HER, He sees HER for all she is and all she can be. He knew exactly who she was, her issues and her problems, and still stopped, just for her and lovingly called her "daughter" (Mark 5:34). When each of us understands that we are loved just like she was loved, we can walk through any crowd with our heads held high, our eyes on Jesus.

So keep walking. Keep showing up. Own and love your story, and look to Christ when you are unsure of where you belong. He will remind you that you are His.

———

Exercise #1

Study women in the gospel whose stories are very different from the "ideal," or find someone in your own ward or life who seems to have had a winding path. Note how the Lord used her to fulfill special purposes.

_____

_____

_____

_____

Exercise #2

Is there someone in your sphere of influence who feels a little different or on the fringe? Make a point to let her know that she is welcomed and loved by you.

_____

_____

_____

_____

If you believe in Jesus, redemption is the only story.

CHAPTER 18

He Suffered For You

When we are progressing and feeling steady, it seems there is always something right around the corner, ready to knock us off our game. Sometimes our mistakes come in small and sneaky ways, derailing us an inch at a time, and other times we take a big step off the path. In those moments, it's easy to convince ourselves that one mess up or a few steps the wrong way means we must distance ourselves from God. That His love and power is only available to those who are perfect or at the very least, exceptionally great.

Do not believe this lie for one minute. Fight it with everything you have. Our Savior is there for us always, at our worst, our weakest, our most rebellious, and our most broken. **The minute we feel that we are undeserving of His love is the exact second we need it the most.**

I have a friend I admire so much for her willingness to do what she can to stay tied to Christ. Many people in her situation walk away, finding it too difficult to teeter between two worlds. But she chooses to stay, even if her life isn't in exact harmony or where she knows it should be. She comes to worship and fellowship and feel of God's love for her and her family. She comes as she is, and we love her for it.

Right now, if you know you love Jesus but are having a hard time holding to the standards or being sure of every piece of doctrine, He wants you anyway, sins, guilt, questions, trials, and all. I love the way Elder Holland put it in his April 2017 talk, "Songs Sung and Unsung": "'Come as you are,' a loving Father says to each of us, but He adds, 'Don't plan to stay as you are.'"[9]

There is a place for you and there always will be, regardless of the way others might see it. The repentance process is personal, and when you are ready, it is all about the Savior's enabling power to work miracles, not just for the women of Galilee, but for your heart today. Your worth, in the eyes of God, does not change because of your choices. You matter to Him just the same.

When Tiger Woods, after years of poor choices,

---

9 Jeffrey R. Holland, "Songs Sung and Unsung."*Ensign, May 2017: https://www.churchofjesuschrist.org/study/general-conference/2017/04/songs-sung-and-unsung?lang=eng*

medical issues, and embarrassing personal problems, came back to win the Masters, people everywhere celebrated. I was among them, using it as an allegory to teach my teens how there is always a way back, and that any time they fail, make mistakes, or disappoint themselves or God, they have the opportunity to be the author of their own comeback story.

As I posted these thoughts on social media, a friend replied, "Is it possible to over-celebrate redemption stories? He hurt a lot of people, and he's basically a hero right now." It only took a couple of seconds before the answer came to my mind. "No. **If you believe in Jesus, redemption is the only story**."

I understood where he was coming from. I remember being a diligent and mostly-obedient teen, reading the story of the Prodigal Son. I thought it was especially unfair that a party was thrown for the kid who had wasted all his money and made poor choices instead of for the brother who had always done things right. I didn't understand how any parent would be happy to have a kid like that come back.

And then I became a parent, and all of a sudden, I got it. I understood the intense love you feel for your children, independent of their choices, and the hope and desire you have for everyone to somehow "return home," even if they are broke and broken when they walk through the door.

The joy of the redemption story doesn't minimize or lessen the love and gratitude you feel for the ones who have constantly and quietly done the right thing. It doesn't erase the growth, trust, and opportunities they have been given because of good choices and a clean life. They might not be the heroes of the moment, but there are more important, more lasting rewards that await.

Redemption also doesn't erase the heartache, the embarrassment, the difficult lessons, and the pain felt by the prodigal son and those who loved him along the way. After the party, there will still be a lifetime of reconciliation and forgiveness to follow. It is a longer, harder road than most of us get to see in one evening party or on 60-second highlight reels.

Our redemption story may not play out under the hot lights of a media frenzy or in the vivid color of primetime TV, but it unfolds in our ordinary lives, inside the protective walls of our homes, or in the quiet corners of our hearts. There comes a time when we all will need a fresh start, a do-over, a Savior.

I think the world loves redemption stories because they remind us all that someone above is rooting for us. That there is a bigger, greater power that wants us all to succeed. And when we fall short of our potential, when we squander our time and talents on things of little worth, when we turn our back on those who need us most, when we forget who we are and where we come from, our Heavenly Parents are still waiting in the doorway with arms outstretched, ready to welcome us back with all the love we don't feel we deserve.

So, I ask myself again, "Is it possible to over-celebrate redemption stories?"

My emphatic answer? "No, never."

So if you are on the fringe, if you are teetering between full fellowship and a quiet exit, can I urge you to keep coming, keep working, keep trying? I believe **there is no better place to rediscover your worth than on your own path to discipleship**, no matter how long that path is, or how far down you have strayed. The world might shout that more is required for you to deserve His love, people might shun you because of what they think they know, but do not listen. Jesus is always ready and waiting for you.

When we open our hearts to this reality, we become women who learn from others instead of comparing ourselves to them; we create holy habits and stay close to Jesus even through questions; we find our worth through God, not through the actions of our family members; we love and accept our bodies as instruments for good; we recognize our spiritual gifts and let Heavenly Father help us develop them; we choose not to judge and instead offer grace; we refuse to define ourselves by outside achievements and accolades; we connect with others and God in meaningful ways every day.

We become women who understand that change is always possible in ourselves and others; we give space for differences and celebrate them; we focus on "the one"; we abandon perfectionist ideals that stifle us in favor of small improvements and growth; we aren't afraid to be still; we forgive with an open heart; we wait and trust in the Lord's timing; we embrace our reality; and we fully believe in redemption through Christ.

In short, we become the women we were always meant to be.

During that day in Galilee, Jesus was on His way to raise the daughter of Jarius from the dead. He had a plan, something important on the docket, but He stopped for our lowly woman because she came looking for Him, and that was all the effort He needed. He wasn't too busy to acknowledge her heart, understand her intent, and openly heal her body and soul, even when the onlookers questioned Him. He fixed His eyes on her, and changed her forever. He will do the same for each of us, if we let Him.

Exercise #1

Is there something you need to repent for that hasn't been cleared up? Start using the Atonement tonight and reflect on true forgiveness.

_____

_____

_____

_____

Exercise #2

Has there been a time when you have felt loved and accepted by Jesus Christ even when you weren't perfect? Journal about that experience or share it with others.

_____

_____

_____

_____

Author's Note

I couldn't end this book without saying thank you to you, the reader. Thank you for going on this journey with an open mind and a willing heart. My hope is that you found in these pages an affirmation of your own worth and goodness, peace in your current circumstances, and a desire to be all you were created to be. I will never be able to adequately express my gratitude to you for trusting me with your time and attention, for letting me into your life.

I hope we can stay connected in the future. You can find me online at brookeromney.com or on Facebook and Instagram @brookeromneywrites. If you are interested in having me join you at a book club or speaking event or have a question, please email me at hello@brookeromney.com. I would love to be part of your book club discussions online or in person, and am more than willing to answer questions and dig deeper with you.

If you found the message of the book important, you can help me tremendously by recommending the book to your family and friends or posting a review online. These small things mean more than you will ever know to an independent author, and I will never be able to repay you for your support.

All my love,

Brooke

Acknowledgements

When I set out to write a book, I had no idea how much support it would take to bring it into existence. Every person who read or discussed it with me is a part of the final copy, and it would never have been completed without them.

Thank you to Morgan Jones, Emily Orton, and Elise Caffee for being my first readers. They gave me the confidence I needed at the very beginning to feel my message was worth pursuing; to Michelle Torsak for the hours she spent reading, for pushing me to make the manuscript better and more inclusive, and for her willingness to go to bat for me; to Tammy Hall for making sure I had my scriptures and Hebrew background right, for making the book as a whole so much more enjoyable to read, and for being the girl you want in your corner. Thank you to Jen Poulton and Katie Park for the hours on the phone convincing me I could make it work and for reading and giving me the boost I needed when I was wavering; and to Chrislyn Woolston for pushing me to get outside my box.

A huge helping of gratitude goes to Anthony Sweat

and David Butler who listened to my ideas, gave me important publishing information, and encouraged me through disappointments. To Miranda Anderson who was incredibly generous with her

time, knowledge, and experience and helped convince me that I really could self-publish a book and that all the effort would be worth it. Without these conversations, there is no way I would have something in print today.

I cannot thank Jane Clayson Johnson enough for her time and attention to detail. She improved the manuscript so much and helped create something significantly better than it was before.

I can credit Emily Belle Freeman with the book's new structure and focus which made it 100% more accessible and relevant. She went above and beyond to ensure that what women have in their hands will make a difference in their daily life. I will never be able to repay her abundant and giving spirit but hope to pay it forward. I know she didn't have time for all she did, but she made time for me, and the finished product has so much to do with her expertise and talent.

My editing team was phenomenal. They were honest, intelligent, and incredible at their craft but also allowed me to stay true to my voice and vision. They helped me create something I am intensely proud of, and I would recommend Carly Springer, Laney Hawes, Bethany Petersen, and Lanae Carmichael to anyone. In addition to them, Derek Campbell from Mix at 6 Studios walked me through and recorded my audiobook and put me at such ease. He created a phenomenal final product with his skill and experience.

I am not sure there is anyone more gifted at design than Mark Romney. He took what I could only envision in my mind and made it a reality. He is intuitive and exact, and his ideas and suggestions blew me away every time. Not only that, but he convinced me that my voice was needed in this saturated world. He has been an incredible encourager of my work.

Thank you to my friends on Instagram who gave input on the title, cover, and design of the book. Crowdsourcing was exciting and gave me a title and cover better than I ever could have come up with on my own. The excitement and support I felt from my community there was humbling and inspiring. My advanced readers came from that group, and they have been so wise and insightful during the publication process.

I cannot thank my close friends and family enough for being the inspiring people they are. They have given opinions on everything I have asked and lived lives worth emulating and writing about. They have picked up my slack when I have been overwhelmed and have been more excited for me than I deserve. I cannot name them all, but you know who you are and I love you more than you know.

I am so grateful for the support of my in-laws and their willingness to be part of this process. They have cheered me along and been engaged and involved from afar. It is so wonderful to have people in my life that encourage me to pursue my passion. I am so grateful to be a Romney and part of their family.

If you read the book, you know that my parents are phenomenal. The older I get, the more I realize how blessed I was to be raised by two people who were so motivated, grounded, and still so full of love. I am only the person I am today because they believed in me from the very beginning and have continued to support and love me as an adult in all the ways that matter most. They are good to the core and quietly make this world a better place.

To my boys: You four have taught me more about

love, goodness, resilience, and forgiveness than I ever thought there was to know. You are each incredible in your own unique way, and being your mom is the greatest gift I have ever been given. I absolutely love walking this road with you and watching you discover more of who you really are every day. Your support of me over the last year has been selfless, and your excitement for what I do and love is an inspiring example to me. Thank you each for being you and for loving me with all my quirks, faults, and horrible renditions of songs you love. I adore you.

And to Mike, who is and always has been my biggest cheerleader, I could never have done this without you. From the very beginning of our life together, you forced me to get out of my comfort zone and become more than I ever knew I wanted to be. You challenge me and support me and never let me get too comfortable, and I am incredibly grateful for that. You are the most selfless person I know; you love people and God so deeply, you make me want to do the same. Thank you for your patience as I figure out myself and for your listening ear while I talk way too much. I cannot imagine going through this life without your steady hand by my side. You make life fun and adventurous and are the kind of man I hope our boys become. From day one, you have loved me with such goodness and devotion, I have always felt like the luckiest woman on Earth, and we sure have a good time together...even after all these years. Thank you for reading and editing and for picking up the slack at home so I could finish what I felt called to do. You have always pushed me to pursue my dreams and I am so grateful for that.

Finally, I must thank my Heavenly Father for the outpouring of inspiration I have felt almost daily for the last year. This book is only because of Him, and I am just honored to be the scribe.

———————

About The Author

Brooke Romney is a writer, speaker, educator, and connector. She has been published in The Washington Post, The Deseret News, Scary Mommy, and a host of other online publications where her pieces have been read millions of times. She writes avidly on her blog and Instagram page where she has created a large, vibrant community of learning and growth. She is currently on the "Time Out for Women" speaking circuit and touches large audiences with her message of worth, empowerment, and connection. She regularly uses her education and expertise to help individuals, online accounts, and businesses tell their stories through a compelling and inviting narrative that positions them for success. "I Like Me Anyway: Embracing Imperfection, Connection, and Christ" is her first book.

Find Brooke online at brookeromney.com or on Instagram and Facebook @brookeromneywrites.

BROOKE ROMNEY Writes

Made in USA - North Chelmsford, MA
1248309_9781735854403
05.25.2021 0956